Volume VII

Report No. 78

March, 1970

The Field of
Family Therapy

Formulated by
the Committee on the Family

Group for the Advancement of Psychiatry

Standard Book Number 87318–107–7

Library of Congress Catalog Card Number 62-2872

Printed in the United States of America

In Memoriam

ALICE ROBERTA CORNELISON

1918–1967

This report is dedicated to the memory of Alice Roberta Cornelison, who served as a consultant to the GAP Committee on the Family from 1955 until shortly before her death on June 16, 1967. A graduate of Vassar College, Miss Cornelison received the degree of M.S.S. from the Smith College School for Social Work. Her long and distinguished participation at Yale in the study of families of schizophrenics is widely recognized and appreciated.

Her contributions to the work of the Committee have been invaluable, and its members deeply regret that she has been prevented from seeing this study reach publication. After such a long and productive association with a treasured friend, the entire Committee shares the heartfelt conviction of one of its members, Dr. Murray Bowen, who wrote to her shortly before her death, "A GAP meeting without you is hard to comprehend."

Table of Contents

This is the ninth in a series of publications comprising Volume VII. For a list of other GAP publications on topics related to this subject, please see page 646.

STATEMENT OF PURPOSE

THE GROUP FOR THE ADVANCEMENT OF PSYCHIATRY has a membership of approximately 300 psychiatrists, most of whom are organized in the form of a number of working committees. These committees direct their efforts toward the study of various aspects of psychiatry and the application of this knowledge to the fields of mental health and human relations.

Collaboration with specialists in other disciplines has been and is one of GAP's working principles. Since the formation of GAP in 1946 its members have worked closely with such other specialists as anthropologists, biologists, economists, statisticians, educators, lawyers, nurses, psychologists, sociologists, social workers, and experts in mass communication, philosophy, and semantics. GAP envisages a continuing program of work according to the following aims:

1. To collect and appraise significant data in the field of psychiatry, mental health, and human relations;
2. To re-evaluate old concepts and to develop and test new ones;
3. To apply the knowledge thus obtained for the promotion of mental health and good human relations.

GAP is an independent group and its reports represent the composite findings and opinions of its members only, guided by its many consultants.

THE FIELD OF FAMILY THERAPY *was formulated by the Committee on the Family.* The members of this committee as well as all other committees are listed below.*

---

* At the time this report was formulated by the Committee on the Family, it was under the chairmanship of Dr. Israel Zwerling. The present members of the Committee wish to express their indebtedness to the following consultants who contributed to the development of ideas for this work: Mr. Jay Haley, Mrs. Celia Mitchell, and Dr. Elmer Struening. We also wish to thank Dr. Suzanne R. Fried, a Sol W. Ginsburg Fellow, for her valuable assistance to the Committee.

526

COMMITTEE ON THE FAMILY
Norman L. Paul, Cambridge, Chr.
Ivan Boszormenyi-Nagy, Philadelphia
Murray Bowen, Chevy Chase
David Mendell, Houston
Joseph Satten, Topeka
Kurt O. Schlesinger, San Francisco
John P. Spiegel, Waltham, Mass.
Lyman C. Wynne, Bethesda
Israel Zwerling, New York

COMMITTEE ON ADOLESCENCE
Joseph D. Noshpitz, Washington, Chr.
Warren J. Gadpaille, Denver
Mary O'Neil Hawkins, New York
Charles A. Malone, Philadelphia
Silvio J. Onesti, Jr., Boston
Vivian Rakoff, Toronto
Jeanne Spurlock, Nashville
Sidney L. Werkman, Denver

COMMITTEE ON AGING
Jack Weinberg, Chicago, Chr.
Robert N. Butler, Washington, D.C.
Lawrence F. Greenleigh, Los Angeles
Maurice E. Linden, Philadelphia
Prescott W. Thompson, San Jose, Calif.
Montague Ullman, Brooklyn

COMMITTEE ON CHILD PSYCHIATRY
E. James Anthony, St. Louis, Chr.
James M. Bell, Canaan, N.Y.
H. Donald Dunton, New York
Joseph M. Green, Madison, Wis.
John F. Kenward, Chicago
William S. Langford, New York
John F. McDermott, Jr., Honolulu
Suzanne T. van Amerongen, Boston
Exie E. Welsch, New York
Virginia N. Wilking, New York

COMMITTEE ON COLLEGE STUDENT
Robert L. Arnstein, New Haven, Chr.
Harrison P. Eddy, New York
Alfred Flarsheim, Chicago
Alan Frank, Albuquerque, N.M.
Malkah Tolpin Notman, Brookline, Mass.

Kent E. Robinson, Towson, Md.
Earle Silber, Chevy Chase, Md.
Tom G. Stauffer, Scarsdale, N.Y.

COMMITTEE ON GOVERNMENTAL
AGENCIES
Harold Rosen, Baltimore, Chr.
Calvin S. Drayer, Philadelphia
Edward O. Harper, Cleveland
John E. Nardini, Washington, D.C.
Donald B. Peterson, Fulton, Mo.

COMMITTEE ON INTERNATIONAL
RELATIONS
Byrant M. Wedge, West Medford, Mass.,
  Chr.
Francis F. Barnes, Chevy Chase
Eugene B. Brody, Baltimore
William D. Davidson, Washington, D.C.
Joseph T. English, Washington, D.C.
Louis C. English, Pomona, N.Y.
Frank Fremont-Smith, Massapequa, N.Y.
Robert L. Leopold, Philadelphia
John A. P. Millet, New York
Alain J. Sanseigne, New York
Bertram Schaffner, New York
Mottram P. Torre, New Orleans
Ronald Wintrob, Hartford

COMMITTEE ON MEDICAL EDUCATION
David R. Hawkins, Charlottesville,Chr.
Hugh T. Carmichael, Washington, D.C.
Robert S. Daniels, Chicago
Raymond Feldman, Boulder, Colo.
Saul I. Harrison, Ann Arbor
Harold I. Lief, Philadelphia
John E. Mack, Boston
William L. Peltz, Philadelphia
David S. Sanders, Los Angeles
Robert A. Senescu, Albuquerque, N.M.
Roy M. Whitman, Cincinnati

COMMITTEE ON
MENTAL HEALTH SERVICES
Lee G. Sewall, N. Little Rock, Ark., Chr.
Eugene M. Caffey, Jr., Washington, D.C.
Morris E. Chafetz, Boston

INTRODUCTION

The rapid growth of family therapy, both as a form of psychotherapeutic practice and as a conceptual approach to psychopathology, has been one of the most remarkable developments in psychiatry and the nonmedical mental health professions over the past two decades. Haley,[1] Spiegel and Bell,[2] Jackson and Satir,[3] and Zuk and Rubinstein[4] have traced the history of this growth and have offered reviews of the burgeoning literature. The frequency with which papers on family therapy find their way into programs at meetings of psychiatric and allied professional organizations, the increasing numbers of centers that offer training in family process and family treatment, and the evident congeniality of both the technique and the approach with the practices and the principles associated with the community psychiatry movement are indications that family therapy has become a firmly established practice in the repertoire of the mental health professional.

This report is offered in response to a need for an overview of the field—a snapshot, so to speak, of the present state of the art —and is intended to answer the following questions:

---

[1] Jay Haley, "Whither Family Therapy," *Family Process,* 1:69–100, 1962.

[2] John P. Spiegel and Norman W. Bell, "The Family of the Psychiatric Patient," in AMERICAN HANDBOOK OF PSYCHIATRY, Vol. 1, Silvano Arieti, ed., Basic Books, Inc., New York, 1959.

[3] Don D. Jackson and Virginia Satir, "A Review of Psychiatric Developments in Family Diagnosis and Family Therapy," in EXPLORING THE BASE FOR FAMILY THERAPY, Nathan W. Ackerman, et al., eds., Family Service Association of America, New York, 1961.

[4] Gerald H. Zuk and David Rubinstein, "A Review of Concepts in the Study and Treatment of Families of Schizophrenics," in INTENSIVE FAMILY THERAPY: THEORETICAL AND PRACTICAL ASPECTS, Ivan Boszormenyi-Nagy and James L. Framo, eds., Harper & Row, New York, 1965.

1. Who are the practitioners of family therapy, by professional discipline and by demographic characteristics, and what influenced them to become family therapists?
2. Who are the patients, and how did they get into family therapy?
3. What are the goals pursued in family therapy, and what indications and contraindications are applied to the selection or rejection of patients for family therapy?
4. What conceptual approaches are used by family therapists in their thinking about treatment programs?
5. What techniques are utilized in the conduct of family therapy programs?
6. From what points of view do therapists conduct family treatment?
7. What ethical problems are encountered in the practice of family therapy?

In the chapters that follow, each of these questions is treated in turn.

The field of family therapy is expanding rapidly both in numbers of practicing professionals and in varieties of practice. Any snapshot of an entity in rapid change is likely to be blurred. Furthermore, another snapshot taken shortly after would likely reveal a significantly different picture. A report on techniques in a stable, well-established practice would have a good chance of retaining its relevance for a decade; a report on family therapy, which is in a *state of rapid transition,* is likely to be quickly superseded.

Progress in the state of the art, then, will very quickly make this report historically rather than operationally useful. Its contributors, however, have made every effort to assure that it is a full and accurate reflection of the field during the winter of 1966–67. These contributors represent all three major mental health disciplines and all major geographic areas in the United

States. Those who participated in this effort not only are themselves active in the field of family therapy, but have frequently visited major psychiatric teaching and training centers and seen at first hand the emergence of new developments. One contributor, as editor of *Family Process,* has visited and observed ongoing work in virtually every center in the country where family therapy is taught. The preparation of this report has involved a careful review of the literature and of the papers presented at the several symposia on family therapy within the last few years. Appendix 1 includes a bibliography of 200 articles and books specifically addressed to family therapy, excluding the vast literature of anthropology, sociology, and social psychology on family structure, organization, and process. A questionnaire, reproduced as Appendix 2, was distributed to 520 persons attending regional and national meetings of their professional organizations,* and the responses of the 312 persons who filled in the questionnaire have been analyzed.

To appreciate the purposes of this report, one should keep these questionnaire data in their appropriate perspective. It was *not* intended, nor would it be feasible now, to address the entire population of family therapists or to designate a statistically representative sample of them. It is, therefore, *not* intended that the numerical tabulations be interpreted as reflecting actual distribution of responses among all mental health professionals engaged in the practice of family therapy during the period February 1966 to February 1967, when the questionnaires were completed. Rather, it was intended: (1) to gather information about a very broad range of therapists, families in therapy, practices, concepts, and problems so that practitioners who had not published and whose work was not generally known could contribute information; and (2) to make a preliminary probe, very

---

* All persons attending sessions or panels that included papers on topics involving the family at the annual meetings of the American Orthopsychiatric Association and the American Psychiatric Association in 1966 were invited to fill out questionnaires, as were individual subscribers to *Family Process.*

tentative at best, into the demography and sociology of family therapy for the identification of problems that might require more refined study. The high percentage of returns, particularly in view of the large effort required to complete the questionnaire, and the substantial number of respondents increase our confidence that we have realized these dual objectives. Thus, it is not a statistically reliable datum that only 1.4 per cent of all mental health professionals practicing family therapy are child psychiatrists; but the fact that so low a percentage of our respondents are from this discipline may point toward a problem that merits more detailed study.

The Individual Versus the Family

The questionnaire data add evidence to the committee's observation of one phenomenon that is currently of vital importance to all of psychiatry: the dilemma of the individual in the social group. Clearly, a schism has developed between two separate points of view. Some practitioners continue to perceive and treat as the central issue in psychopathology the disequilibrium in the intrapsychic apparatus of the patient, viewing the contextual social matrix of development and adaptation—and most particularly the family—as adding an important dimension to their conceptualization and treatment. Others see and treat as the central issue the disequilibrium in the family, viewing the altered balance of intrapsychic forces and counterforces in an individual to be of secondary or even of inconsequential relevance to the task of the helping professional. In our experience as well as among our respondents, the greater number falls into the former category. These continue to practice individual psychotherapy or psychoanalysis along with their practice of family therapy and ascribe varying weights to the relative importance each plays in any particular case. A significant minority fall into the second category; some members of this group treat individual persons, but this is undertaken in the context of effecting a change in the family process. This group appears to include the larger number of experienced family therapists; whether experience led them to their conceptual approach or vice versa cannot be determined by our data, though it seems likely that both situations are represented. We judge that the majority of therapists fall between these two extreme positions. The shift in perspective from the individual to the family as the unit of study and treatment seems quite consistent with the broader trend in social psychiatry toward field approaches and to the application of general systems theory. This issue is discussed in detail in Chapter Six.

There are a number of trends in family therapy that are similar to trends in individual therapy. There is, for example, a striking gap between theory and practice; the conceptual approach formulated by the family therapist bears only a tenuous relationship to his actual conduct of treatment. This report focuses principally on what family therapists report they do rather than on their theories of families. Many initial attempts at family therapy reflect a desperate search for *any* effort to bring about change in refractory cases, and success is then followed by the extension of the approach to less experimental settings, until practice finally occurs in private offices and with minimally disabled patients. Finally, family therapy tends to make explicit what often remains implicit or even covert in individual therapy. This is perhaps best illustrated in the many ethical issues that emerge when the therapist, with his goals and anticipations, contracts to treat a patient who also has goals and anticipations. The therapist for an individual may say that his responsibility is only to his patient. This reasoning is challenged when the therapist is confronted by a family in which the identified "patient" may be the least disabled of the family unit. The individual therapist, as he is often unaware of the consequent chain reaction of behaviors from patient to sibling or from patient to any other family member, assumes that what is good for the patient is inherently good for the rest of the family.

1

THE THERAPIST'S ROUTE
TO FAMILY THERAPY

For some years family doctors, clergymen, and marriage counselors have often used a family approach to problems of people. Family therapy as such, however, has only more recently begun to be clearly defined, not only as a method of treatment but also as a theoretical orientation toward psychiatric problems. This chapter attempts to describe family therapists as this group is known to us at centers at which we work and have visited. Further data were provided by those who responded to the committee's questionnaire. While we are quite uncertain about the bias of our sampling procedures, we feel that the data concerning the practitioners themselves are substantially in accord with our experience. Although the term "family therapist" will be used, it is not meant to imply that these therapists practice family therapy exclusively. Most consider family therapy one of several possible treatment methods and ways of understanding psychiatric problems.

The backgrounds of people doing family therapy, their training, and their experience are quite varied. Many disciplines are represented, at least as many as among other types of psychotherapists. In our questionnaire sample, most fall into three groups: social workers, psychiatrists, and psychologists. Social workers make up the largest single group, about 40 per cent, and psychiatrists and psychologists together account for another 40 per cent. Among the remaining are marriage counselors, clergymen, nonpsychiatric physicians, child psychiatrists, nurses, sociologists, and others from scattered discipline. Despite the many social workers in our sample, men outnumber women by two to one. It is our impression that the wide range of professionals practicing family therapy is partly the result of the theoretical model used in family therapy, with relatively little emphasis placed on the classical medical model. People from varied disciplines, particularly nonmedical disciplines, find such a model more comfortable to work with, more "interesting" and more "enjoyable." At the same time such a model probably in turn reflects the varied backgrounds and orientations of the people working in this field, who have developed the theories and techniques.

There is no uniform religious affiliation of family therapists; virtually all faiths are represented in our experience and in our sample, which includes many with no religious affiliations. Very few therapists, regardless of their religious affiliation, ascribe a religious motivation to their conducting family therapy.

Of the 297 respondents who gave their ages, about 80 per cent are 49 years old or under:

Age	Frequency	Percentage of All Respondents
25–29	18	6.1
30–34	58	19.5
35–39	56	18.9
40–44	65	21.9
45–49	41	13.8
50–54	27	9.1
55–59	18	6.1
60 and over	14	4.7
Total	297	100.1

An older therapist experienced in a particular orientation and treatment modality is not very likely to change this radically.

He has already developed a style and a conceptual framework in which to view his work, and with which he is relatively comfortable. For a younger therapist, the practice of family therapy does not involve a large change. Indeed, a number answering our questionnaire had had some experience with family therapy during training. Our average respondent had not had much more experience with any other orientation or style. Although many who practice family therapy reported receiving training during their graduate or postgraduate studies, many others did not.

There is apparently no decisive set of circumstances associated with initiating a therapist's interest in family therapy. Some reported that they responded to a formal training program; others, to a lecture or paper, or to watching a family therapist work. Often some direct contact was involved with one of the pioneers in family therapy, such as Ackerman, Bowen, Satir, or Jackson. Some decided to try family therapy as a result of their work with several individuals of one family. Less often their interest in family therapy was sparked by an invitation from colleagues to explore it. Usually it was a combination of circumstances that led to a therapist's interest in family therapy.

Previous work experience has also influenced the decision about whether to practice family therapy. For some respondents, previous work with groups or schizophrenic patients was thought to be of importance. A majority of family therapists reported having been dissatisfied with the results of individual treatment. A majority also consider themselves to have "general experimental curiosity."

Many family therapists have also had a previous interest in marriage and the family, which certainly had some influence on their decision. Many others were interested and had had experience in treating children and their parents, although only a few are child psychiatrists. Other considerations reported to have had varying importance in motivating family therapists include involvement in a research project, job demands, and personal interest arising from their own family experience. Clearly then, previous interest and work experiences have been associated in a variety of ways with an individual's interest in family therapy— probably in as many ways as there have been different experiences; and almost always it is a combination of influences that has led to this decision. The one factor, however, that is of somewhat greater importance to more family therapists than any others mentioned is a desire to treat people more efficiently. Among the respondents to the questionnaire, for example, 90 per cent felt this to be the most important influence, and almost 65 per cent listed it as their first, second, or third most important influence.

It seems to be an almost universal feeling among the respondents that family therapy is more effective, and that results can be seen more quickly and often more clearly. They are comfortable with the method and feel that it "makes sense" theoretically. Although it is usually not practiced exclusively, it is felt to be the preferred treatment for certain families. The overwhelming majority indicated their intention to continue to maintain a role for family therapy in their treatment repertoire.

2

THE FAMILY'S ROUTE TO FAMILY THERAPY

There is no doubt that during the past few years there has been a growing interest in family therapy. Although only 26 per cent of the respondents answered the question about numbers of referrals, 48 percent of those who did reported an increase in the referrals they received over the preceding year; only 2 per cent reported a decrease; the remainder indicated no change. It would appear that more and more people, laymen and professionals, are learning of this innovative method and are turning to it as a means of working through psychological problems. Another indication of this growing interest is the increase in programs and workshops focused on family therapy at professional conferences.

Section II.3 of the questionnaire (Appendix 2) sought to ascertain the sources of referrals among our respondents. The following table indicates the percentages of family therapists who reported receiving referrals from each of several medical sources.

Medical Sources	*Percentage of Respondents Receiving Referrals*
Psychiatrist	58
General practitioner	51
Pediatrician	33
Internist	31
Psychoanalyst	25

These percentages include any level of referral from a few to many cases. These figures suggest that, despite their tradition of the individual-patient model, psychiatrists and psychoanalysts are frequent endorsers of a family therapy approach. It sometimes happens that these professionals will use family therapists as consultants to individual therapy when they encounter impasses in treatment because of family conflicts or resistances. Occasionally, when there is a family involved with several therapists for its individual members, a family therapist becomes necessary to integrate this network of therapies and to consult with those family members not under treatment.

The interest of general practitioners in family therapy is significant. When the general practitioner treats illnesses for the entire family, he often becomes aware of conflicts and tensions in family interrelationships and is likely to look toward family therapy as a possible remedy. Because of this, a number of postgraduate courses in family mental health and pathology have been evolved to broaden the skill of the general practitioner. To educate the nonpsychiatric physician in matters of family psychotherapy, innovative approaches have been developed to teach family medicine to the medical student to enhance his clinical skills. "Psychiatric Family Consultations," by Treusch and Grotjahn,* outlines a technique by which a family physician can utilize family therapy to understand better the interdependence between some physical disorders and relationships among family members.

Of the community sources for referrals to family therapists, the school was most frequently reported (by 54 per cent). Thirty-nine per cent reported referrals from the police or court, and 34 per cent reported referrals from a church. These figures suggest which community organizations are turning toward family therapy and why. The school, for example, deals not only with

---

* See Bibliography, Appendix 1.

students but also with their parents in reporting on student progress and soliciting conferences for the review of problems. Thus the school often becomes aware of family problems and, in making recommendations for psychiatric therapy, would be likely to prefer a treatment mode that could encompass both the student and his family. Both the police and the court deal with altercations between spouses and delinquents and, to some extent, with families that nurture these problems. They are thus inclined to view family therapy as a means for ameliorating such problems. Church referrals may reflect an increased awareness in pastoral counselors of the relationship between individual distress and family difficulties.

Surprisingly, only 19 per cent of our respondents reported referrals from the children's agencies, and only 10 per cent from residential centers for children. This may suggest that child-oriented treatment centers tend to cling to the traditional focus on the child's pathology. The fact that many of the children under their care come from fragmented and severely disturbed families with a low level of child-caring capability may preclude consideration of family therapy by social workers and therapists at such institutions. There is a growing awareness, however, that children in placement tend to replicate their parents' behavior later in their lives and eventually place their own children. Some placement agencies, therefore, have endeavored to prevent placement by providing multiple therapeutic services to the entire family and, where placement is unavoidable, to work with the family toward the eventual reintegration of the extruded child into the family.

Responses to the questionnaire indicated a number of self-referrals, that is, patients seeking family therapy on their own initiative after hearing of it from other patients or from the mass media. Thirty-eight per cent of the families were reported to have requested family therapy for themselves, including 21 per cent who had heard of it from other families, 9 per cent who had learned of it from newspapers or magazines, and 8 per cent whose information had come from TV or radio. The potential use of mass media for bringing to public attention the concepts and possibilities of all modes of therapy has scarcely been explored and merits careful consideration. Furthermore, none of the respondents, all caretakers, were questioned about the influence of mass media on themselves. It might also be useful to assess the potentialities of these media for increasing awareness of therapeutic modalities and innovative approaches among caretaking professionals.

A cautious note in this connection is necessary. The evidence of family disorder and breakdown, the extent of youthful unrest, rebellion, and alienation from the parental generation is so great that people in need will clutch at any straw. It is, therefore, essential in utilizing the mass media not to make unrealistic claims for the family approach or to "oversell" it. If the public's expectations for services promising some degree of success are stimulated unrealistically and then disappointed, psychiatry can expect a backlash. Whether through the mass media or any other educational approach, the newness of the method has to be acknowledged and its goals made as clear as possible. Precisely because the treatment of the family unit offers a link that has been missing between the individual and the community, it seems to "make sense" for many people, yet it need not be presented as a panacea, a substitute for all other approaches, or even appropriate in all cases as a total self-contained service. This is particularly important at this time when community-based psychiatric services are being set up and expanded everywhere and the use of the family therapy approach promises to be among the major services of community psychiatry.

In respect to the decision to employ family therapy as a mode of treatment, almost 75 per cent of the respondents indicated that, in over two-thirds of their cases, their evaluation of the presenting problem was a major consideration. Most of the respondents indicated that, for half of their cases, individual treatment developed into family therapy. There were fewer reports of moving from the treatment of a marital pair to the treatment of the whole family, possibly because of spontaneous improvements in children accompanying a stabilization of the marital situation, or possibly because therapists working with marital pairs tend to overlook the family context of which the marital relationship is one subsystem. Since the number of respondents who answered this question (II.4) was considerably smaller than the total population of respondents, any assessment of the data should await a follow-up, perhaps in two or three years.

These data indicate that family therapy is beginning to have an impact on both professionals and laymen. Community institutions and medical men are recommending it more frequently; patients are learning about it from other families and from mass media. Yet other responses indicate that the acceptance of this mode of treatment is, at best, gradual. Respondents were asked about the settings for their family treatment: private practice, research or training project, pastoral or school setting, or mental health facility. Of the 1187 families reported on in this part of the questionnaire, only 2 per cent were seen under the auspices of a training project. This suggests that our sample consists primarily of service-oriented practitioners who rarely teach family therapy. Most training institutions do not provide this kind of teaching in their curriculum.

Only 3 per cent of the sample indicated that they were involved in research—another indication that family therapy is, at this point, almost exclusively the province of service programs with few efforts toward controlled studies. The sample included no students in psychiatric social work, though both psychology and psychiatry were represented at the student level.

The Slow Growth of Family Therapy

The questionnaire yielded other data that attest to the slow growth of family therapy. Forty-eight per cent of the therapists in private practice who responded were treating only 16 per cent of the families reported on; nearly half of the practitioners saw only one or two families each week. Obviously, caretaking professionals are slowly acquainting themselves with this approach. The total number of families and couples treated by these respondents is slightly in excess of the total number of persons seen in individual psychotherapy. Although these therapists are using family therapy, they lean strongly on the traditional individual treatment mode. This pluralistic approach of the respondents, using both individual and family therapy, indicates a period of transition and experimentation in therapeutic practice.

Figures on diagnostic evaluations were significantly low. Thirty-five per cent of the therapists practicing family therapy, 19 per cent of those treating couples, and 22 per cent of those seeing individuals performed diagnostic evaluations during the preceding 12 months. It appears that this minority of professionals do diagnostic evaluations only when referring various units to other professionals for treatment. Or, perhaps many who treat families, couples, and individuals do not think in terms of diagnostic evaluation but rather in terms of immediate treatment from their first contact with patients. If, indeed, treatment implies intervention at the very first session, a redefinition of treatment versus diagnosis is needed. This problem is related not only to family therapy but to all forms of treatment.

The whole question of diagnostic evaluation poses an additional problem for the therapist concerned with family or conjoint marital treatment. The traditional terminology used for individuals in individual psychotherapy does not apply to a group of patients. One cannot label the psychological maladaptations of a whole family with one term; the malfunctioning and problems may vary sharply from one member to another. What is needed, then, is a new nomenclature, a new method whereby the problems of an entire family can be diagnosed systematically and validly.

Question II.2 of the questionnaire (Appendix 2) asked those respondents working in mental health facilities to specify the type of the facility. Twenty-one per cent reported that they work in a family service agency; 88 per cent of these are social workers and 4 per cent consulting psychiatrists. Twenty per cent work in community mental health centers; of these, 37 per cent are psychiatrists, 33 per cent social workers, and 18 per cent psychologists. The state hospital ranked third among respondents, followed by the child guidance clinic and the private mental hospital.

It is clear that the family service agency, which formerly treated each family member separately, has begun to see family groups. One reason for this shift in emphasis is the feeling in such agencies that there is a need for more effective and efficient programs to deal with the growing pressures and tensions in the modern family. In November 1967, Clark Blackburn, General Director of the Family Service Association of America, noted in a statement to the press that "service programs need to change to help families successfully cope with their changing environment and personal tensions." He stated that "While individual counseling is still useful for many people, some of the traditional ways of serving families are outmoded." This shift of focus from the individual to the whole family is also reflected in the community mental health center.

Respondents were also asked to specify the number of hours per week they spent at these various mental health facilities. Forty per cent reported 20 hours or less at these settings; 60 per cent reported more than 20 hours; only 3 per cent of the latter group reported more than 40 hours per week. These data suggest that, for many practitioners, work in the public-oriented sector is part-time.

Among all respondents, 46 per cent work in an outpatient service setting, while only 24 per cent work in an inpatient mental health facility. Since in an inpatient service setting the patient is separated from his family and from his community environment, the tendency to use family therapy in the treatment of such a patient is reduced. Family therapy seems more relevant to the outpatient service since it implements the resolution of difficulties with community-related persons, particularly the family. The percentage of respondents working in inpatient services suggests, however, that such institutions are beginning to consider the patient's life in the community and to include the whole family in working toward a resolution of the problem.

Thus, the questionnaire appears to indicate that while family therapy is attracting a good deal of notice and interest, by and large it is still viewed as an innovative approach, mainly the province of caretakers interested in trying new methods and theories. It has not yet become sufficiently established to be included in the curriculum of most teaching institutions or in the treatment orientations of many inpatient services. Thus, most families arrive at family therapy through advice of various caretaking professionals, community organizations, or acquaintances who have been attracted to this innovative therapeutic approach.

One interesting possibility, not at all adequately answered by the questionnaire, is the idea that some turn to family therapy because of failure in other therapeutic modalities, such as individual treatment. It seems possible that some mental health workers, as well as families, who have experienced failure in the use of other more traditional forms would try family therapy simply because it is a different and somewhat new approach. Unfortunately, however, there have been no comprehensive studies made of the incidence of failures and the reasons for them in the different modes of therapy. If such data could be garnered, it might be possible to determine the connection between failure in previous treatment and a consequent interest in family therapy as an innovative approach.

Another important piece of information not solicited in the questionnaire is the social class of the families referred for family therapy. If, as the questionnaire seems to indicate, most family therapy is conducted in a private setting or in an outpatient setting on a part-time basis, it seems possible that this treatment modality would be used primarily for middle-class families, who have the wherewithal to afford a therapist. In addition, such families are more likely to have family doctors, pediatricians, or friends, people who might know about this method. Lower-class families, on the other hand, rely mainly on clinics and may have little exposure to the idea of family therapy and no resources to pay for it anyway. Far more accurate and detailed statistics are needed before it can be ascertained how far down into the social structure family therapy has penetrated.

3

GOALS AND INDICATIONS

It should be obvious to anyone who has ever participated in or observed any form of psychotherapy that there is a considerable difficulty in converting intentions and goals into actual techniques and practices. It is nevertheless useful to try to specify and clarify the avowed goals of family therapists. Such information may add to an understanding of the conceptual framework of family therapists, discussed elsewhere in this report, and to a picture of possible future developments in technique and practice.

A useful distinction can be made between immediate, short-term goals and over-all, long-term goals. The short-term goals will vary over the course of therapy and are typically related to technique in an obvious fashion. On the other hand, the long-term goals and values are much less explicit and may be only partially spelled out in the therapist's thinking and behavior.

Initially, the family therapist typically has the immediate goal of discovering if and how the presenting problem is linked to a definable system of family relationships. In what ways are the family members (and possibly other persons) emotionally and behaviorally involved with each other? Inquiry and observation about *what* concerns the family members will simultaneously give clues as to *who* is involved. Thus, a second immediate goal is to assess who the participants in the family therapy might appropriately be. Both of these immediate goals are related to the interest of the family therapist in the family—as a system in its own right and also as a context for the particular behavior and experience of the individual family members. Family therapists appear to differ in the emphasis they place on these two interests, but most seem to have some concern with both.

A third short-term goal of many family therapists is to show the family members, by confrontation, interpretations, or active interventions, some of the ways in which they are currently involved with one another in the interview situation itself. Some therapists explicitly wish to arouse an interest in continued participation by the family, especially by those family members who at first come compliantly or allegedly only for the sake of the identified patient.

Diversity of Goals

There is a diversity of other short-term goals that feed into the longer-lasting objectives of some family therapists. For example, Satir makes getting each family member to voice a specific comment an immediate goal at the beginning of the first interview, regardless of the content. She feels this serves the purpose of having all the family members "commit themselves to coming not in the interest of the patient but in the interest of themselves" and thus demonstrates that each person has a definite place in the family treatment. This then is the first move toward reaching the longer-term goal of enhancing the individuation of the family members.

Other family therapists have an immediate goal of discovering whether family patterns in which they are especially interested are present, for example, whether there is evidence of empathy and intimacy between the family members, whether they have the capacity to observe and comment upon their own behavior with one another, and whether the family arouses particular kinds of feelings and subjective experiences in the therapist, reactions that he may use for their information value about the family.

Some family therapists see themselves as letting long-term

goals emerge out of the family treatment process itself, so the goals are a *result* of how the therapy unfolds. Other therapists appear to have quite definite long-term goals from the start. If the therapist implicitly or explicitly believes he knows what the family members should do, be, or want, he is apt to be more active from the start in working toward these goals. For example, if he is convinced that clear communication is a primary "good," he may try to induce the family members to sort out and clarify their "messages" to one another. Or, if he is convinced that positive feelings of intimacy are "good" and important, he may pay less attention to clear verbalization and try to evoke positive expressions of feelings by family members. Such therapists are apt to seek a major goal, such as clear communication or greater intimacy, with *all* families, regardless of the presenting problem or the stated wishes of the family members about these goals.

The questionnaire did not attempt to tap the great diversity of possible combinations of goals by family therapists; these are clearly numerous and overlapping. A sampling of goals was listed in the questionnaire under eight headings, designated as either *primary* or *secondary,* and as applying to work with *all* families or with certain families (see Question VI:1, Appendix 2). Two of the listed goals involved changes that are central objectives in most individual psychotherapies: symptomatic improvement in one or more family members and improved task performance by one or more members (e.g., school performance of a child, work performance of a parent). The cardinal goal of psychoanalytic therapy—structural personality change, with symptomatic change regarded as secondary—was not listed as a possibility. Most of the other listed goals involved changes not as directly related to individual family members as to the functioning of the family as a whole. "Improved autonomy and individuation of family members" refers to individual family members rather than to the family as a whole, but it seems quite clear that the implication of this goal from the standpoint of *family* therapy is that there would be individuation of the family members *in relation to each other*.

The overwhelming majority, above 90 per cent, of the 290 respondents answering this section said that they have *all eight* of the stated goals as their own primary or secondary goal with at least some families. On this point, the range of variation was only from that for "improved communication"—not a single respondent said this was rarely or never a goal—to the maximum of only 6 per cent who indicated "symptomatic improvement in one or more family members" was rarely or never a goal. Also, over half of the respondents take as a *primary* goal, either with all or with certain families, *all eight* of the stated goals (see Table 1, column c).

A marked variation in frequency of adopting these goals, however, is apparent if one notes the frequency with which the respondents take the different goals as their *"primary* goal with *all* families." Here the spread is from 85 per cent for "improved communication" to 12 per cent for "improved individual task performance." "Individual symptomatic improvement" is also near the bottom of this list, at the 23 per cent level. Ranking behind "improved communication" at the top of the list are "improved autonomy-individuation" and "improved empathy," both at the 56 per cent level (see Table 1, column a).

In contrast, "individual task performance" and "individual symptomatic improvement" are at the top of the list of *secondary* goals (see Table 2). Thus, it would appear that, in the present sample of family therapists, family-wide change, as in improved communication, is given more stress than change that may occur in only part of the family or in one or more individual family members; but the goal of changing individual symptoms and task performance is by no means abandoned.

It may appear to some that there is a conflict between the goal of improving individual autonomy and differentiation and the practice of bringing the family members together in a conjoint therapeutic effort. This is a dilemma only if the fact of their

TABLE 1

Primary Goals Stated by Therapist
with Families Actually in Treatment (N = 290)

Primary Goals	(a) With all families %	(b) With certian families %	(c) Total %
1. Improved communication	85	5	90
2. Improved autonomy and individuation	56	31	87
3. Improved empathy	56	15	71
4. More flexible leadership	34	32	66
5. Improved role agreement	32	32	64
6. Reduced conflict	23	37	60
7. Individual symptomatic improvement	23	33	56
8. Improved individual task performance	12	38	50

meeting together geographically is taken literally to mean that the family members are thereby expected to fuse somehow psychologically. It does appear to be a fear on the part of some thera-

TABLE 2

Secondary Goals Stated by Therapist
with Families Actually in Treatment (N = 290)

Secondary Goals	(a) With all families %	(b) With certain families %	(c) Total %
1. Improved individual task performance	16	29	45
2. Individual symptomatic improvement	23	15	38
3. Reduced conflict	17	18	35
4. Improved role agreement	17	15	32
5. More flexible leadership	11	19	30
6. Improved empathy	17	8	25
7. Improved autonomy and individuation	7	5	12
8. Improved communication	8	1	9

pists who have never worked with families that differentiation and individuation can only be achieved by a geographic separation. Naturally enough, family therapists, especially those who work with families having a late-adolescent or young-adult offspring, believe on the contrary that genuine individuation and eventual separation can best be achieved by working with the family conjointly so that the patterns and bonds that bind them together can be altered on a fundamental, emotional level.

The therapeutic goals of achieving increased separation versus increased closeness are complicated by the belief that deepened intimacy and closeness are possible only for persons who have achieved some degree of individuation. Some therapists, especially those who work particularly with marital couples, quite frankly believe that a long-standing marriage must have at least some basis for love and satisfaction, even though this may be obscured by bickering and other common pastimes. In contrast, other therapists have an avowed goal of being neutral about whether a family or a married couple should stay together; these therapists often have some primary goal other than improved empathy and intimacy, such as improved communication or improved individuation. They try to trust the family or marital pair to make a sensible choice about staying together or not—hopefully more wisely if they are, for example, communicating more clearly. Some of these therapists deliberately try not to take sides about such matters as impending divorce.

In contrast, some family therapists, equally experienced, take unabashed stands in favor of the continuation of current marriages. Sometimes such "biases" are adopted as a therapeutic device to facilitate the exploration of an aspect of the family life that may otherwise be obscure. Nonetheless, it is undoubtedly true that the value systems and the related long-term goals of various family therapists do show a considerable range in the ways in which they are viewed and expressed.

A more complicated area of present controversy in the field

of family therapy concerns the alternative goals of (1) altering patterns of behavior, especially communicative behavior, versus (2) obtaining access to and altering the subjective experience of the family members in addition to altering their patterns of behavior. A third alternative, that of having the primary goal of trying to alter subjective experience "intrapsychically," is not the avowed goal of any known family therapist. Such goals are sometimes held by existential therapists and by some psychoanalysts who work exclusively with individual patients using an individual, intrapsychic conceptual frame of reference. Actually, even among therapists who see patients only on an individual basis, the contextual framework of the patient's experience is now widely accepted as significant and even fundamental, despite a few continuing doctrinaire pronouncements to the contrary.

Among family therapists, the controversy is a matter of emphasis. At the one extreme, there are those therapists who use communication theory most rigorously and who stress those aspects of behavior that can be objectively heard or observed—those features that would be recorded by electronic devices such as videotape equipment. Therapists who use this method do not necessarily dismiss the importance of existential and subjective experience, but they take the pragmatic stance that the goal of therapy should be to intervene in observable communications and behavior; they assume that changes in subjective experience will result from such interventions. These therapists contend that the results of this approach are superior, that concern with subjective experience is distracting and time-wasting, and that interest in subjective experience represents an atavistic hangover from group affiliation with psychoanalyst and other individually-oriented colleagues.

In contrast, the family therapists who are interested in both behavior and subjective experience tend to emphasize the goal of improved empathy and make use of the impact of the family's behavior on the therapist's experience, for example, what the family does that leaves him feeling confused or despairing, angry, or sexually aware (so-called "countertransference"). These therapists try to make use of what they regard as the empathic resonance between the feeling states of themselves and the family members. They regard this resonance as a significant aspect of the emotional organization of the family as a system. These therapists tend to regard as most meaningful an individual's subjective experience, viewing behavior apart from subjective experience as not very illuminating, indeed even misleading in some circumstances. Thus, they are more interested in encouraging family members to "reveal" themselves in their inner life, to convey to one another and to the therapist something about both joyous and anguished experiences, present and past, especially if the past experience, as with unresolved grief reactions, continues to have reverberations in family life. These therapists are more apt to be observers than active leaders of the family therapy group, and more apt to wait and see what they experience and what is going on, than to move in as quickly and as consistently as the therapists of the first group. The family therapists who have the goal of getting in touch with subjective experience are also interested in communication and observable behavior, but regard this emphasis as incomplete.

The problem of defining goals is complicated not only because the avowed goals of therapists are frequently at variance with what they actually do, but also because their goals may be at odds with the goals of the persons treated. This can be an issue even when the therapist's goal is to assist the family members to individuate in ways of their own choice; persons in disturbed families, especially in families with an identified schizophrenic member, often have a more or less explicit goal of staying or becoming more undifferentiated, of losing themselves in one another. Thus, whatever the goal of the therapist may be, even the goal of individuation, this is likely to be at odds with the goals of some or all members of certain families. This means that the areas of shared goals of therapist and family must necessarily evolve over time; each may shift substantially under the impact of their encounter.

Until recently, very few families came to therapy prepared to share the therapist's goal of exploring how the identified patient's presenting symptoms were a manifestation of family-wide problems. A decade ago, therapists rarely received problems said to be located primarily in the family as a whole, but were instead presented with "a patient" who typically had symptomatic difficulties that more or less sharply differentiated him from other family members. When family therapists introduced to the families of such individuals the concept of troubled *families* rather than troubled *individuals,* they were sometimes surprised to find that certain families were very ready, even eager, to shift to a family frame of reference and quickly immersed themselves in the family therapeutic endeavor. On the other hand, other families, perhaps the majority, continued to "prejudicially scapegoat" their "patient" and to have difficulties in adopting the goal of work with the family as a whole. For many families, and some therapists, the adoption of a family orientation is especially difficult when conspicuous behavior and symptoms have emerged in one or another family member and have resulted in hospitalization, legal charges, school expulsion, etc.—events that may dominate the presenting picture. In these instances, the community as well as the therapist and the family are likely to focus at least temporarily upon the individual, even when it is quite reasonable to infer that the symptomatic difficulties of the individual are a manifestation of more covert problems in the family as a whole. Under such circumstances, the "field" or "system" for therapy may be difficult to define and may include an array of hospital personnel who can usefully participate in the family therapy approach only after considerable special training. This example illustrates how external circumstances may make family therapy impractical, or "contraindicated," even when the same problem under other circumstances might be quite suitable for family therapy.

In principle, the clinical indications for family therapy cover a wide spectrum. It should be noted that a therapist's view of the indications and contraindications will vary with whether he is talking about family therapy defined as the treatment of two or more family members *meeting conjointly,* at least during much of the therapy, or regarding family therapy more broadly as an orientation and alertness to problems of family relationships. Because of various conditions that interfere with seeing more than one family member simultaneously, it is obvious that the indications for the latter approach are more varied.

Writers who have discussed indications and contraindications for family therapy have most often used the former definition and have considered a variety of specific situations in which conjoint family therapy seems preferable, or not, compared to other forms of psychotherapy. That this is a common practice among family therapists is suggested by the response to the questionnaire: 89 per cent stated that their reasons for deciding upon family treatment include consideration of the particular kinds of difficulties that they feel should appropriately be treated with a family approach.

The problem is whether there are indeed particular conditions that respond more easily to family therapy than to other forms of treatment. Unfortunately, there is little or no systematic research that has actually compared alternative approaches with the same kinds of problems. It has been suggested on the basis of clinical impressions that the problems of adolescence involving separation from the family are examples of a condition for which family therapy is especially indicated (Ackerman, Wynne), although the use of individual psychotherapy for the adolescent, in addition to the family therapy, appears to be a commonly recommended combination (Jackson, Shapiro). Marital problems, which are now often presented as such, without either spouse being designated as an identified patient, are of course another special indication. Perhaps the most common, though vague, "indication" for family therapy is the failure of other forms of treatment. Since treatment failures are especially common with schizophrenics and other psychotic patients, with acting-out individuals, and with other persons from lower-class and slum environments, it is not surprising that family therapy has been tried with all of these. A number of family therapists feel encouraged, compared to their previous experiences, particularly with individual psychotherapy, but systematic research assessments are still badly needed in this field, just as with other forms of psychotherapy.

Contraindications for Family Therapy

The chief contraindications for family therapy are conditions that interfere with getting a working relationship with the family established or maintained (Wynne). These include conditions that persistently interfere with the physical or psychological availability of key members of the family constellation, phases of the over-all psychotherapeutic progress in which non-familial relations are in focus, and the unavailability of therapists who are able to develop a workable orientation to families as subsystems and who are able to be flexibly active in the treatment process—more essential than is usually the case in individual therapy.

Looking at the characteristics of certain families, Ackerman* has noted a number of other contraindications for family therapy.

For most of these, it is not that the family therapy approach would be necessarily harmful, but rather that it is likely to be unsuccessful and unworkable, a fate probably shared for these instances with other therapies:

---

* Nathan W. Ackerman, TREATING THE TROUBLED FAMILY, Basic Books, Inc., New York, 1966.

(1) The presence of a malignant, irreversible trend toward the breakup of the family, which may mean that it is too late to reverse the process of fragmentation.

(2) The dominance within the group of a concentrated focus of malignant, destructive motivation.

(3) One parent who is afflicted with an organized, progressive paranoid condition, or with incorrigible psychopathic destructiveness, or who is a confirmed criminal or pervert.

(4) Parents, one or both, who are unable to be sufficiently honest; lying and deceitfulness that are deeply rooted in the group negate the potential usefulness of family therapy.

(5) The existence of a certain kind of valid family secret.

(6) The existence of an unyielding cultural, religious, or economic prejudice against this form of intervention.

(7) The existence in some members of extremely rigid defenses which, if broken, might induce a psychosis, a psychosomatic crisis, or physical assault.

(8) Finally, the presence of organic disease or other disablement of a progressive nature that precludes the participation of one or more members.

Many family therapists do not share this view of contraindications to family therapy, but rather see the issues raised by Ackerman as challenging problems in the conduct of family therapy programs.

In considering the indications for family therapy compared to other types of therapy, most questionnaire respondents (83 per cent) stated that they are interested in comparing the outcome of individual and family approaches for treatment of similar problems, and 85 per cent are concerned with the problem of combining individual therapy with family therapy. In contrast, only 47 per cent ever consider conventional group therapy as an alternative to family therapy. In this sample of people conducting family treatment, there continues to be a very strong concern with the comparative usefulness of individual therapy and a family approach, but relatively little interest in other alternatives.

Although most of the family therapists are interested in such questions, they do not pursue them in systematic research. Rather, the respondents give consideration to these issues on the basis of discussions with colleagues. Only from 8 per cent to 23 per cent of the respondents expressed a research interest in any of 12 listed questions. At the top of the list (23 per cent), was an interest in follow-up assessment, that is, changes taking place after family treatment has ended. Second, 19 per cent have a research interest in how different kinds of intervention can affect the processes of therapy. It does not seem likely that widespread research on family treatment will be forthcoming from our respondents, although family therapy is probably more often directly observed and studied than has been historically true in other forms of psychotherapy.

4

CONCEPTUAL FRAMEWORK

The family therapy "movement" as it has emerged in the United States during the last decade can be considered both as a practical clinical development and as a conceptual revolution. There are various reasons why the movement has raised more questions of theoretical interest than earlier modifications in treatment approaches. Major among these is that those interested in the practice of family therapy are psychotherapists who wish to reach out beyond the limits of the individual approach in psychiatry, or thinkers intrigued with conceptual frameworks involving multi-person or transactional systems, or practitioners who belong to both these categories.

Family therapy did not originate as an attempt to broaden treatment coverage from one to several individuals as group therapy did earlier, even though it is true that conjoint family therapy also accomplishes simultaneous treatment of several persons. The specific contribution of the method has been that it offers the opportunity to work directly with relational contexts rather than to affect individuals isolated from their significant relationships. A main dimension of the group process of family therapy is based on the ongoing feedback of mutually formative relationships that have their existential reality mainly outside the therapy situation. For example, an emancipating adolescent is treated together with the emotionally resistant, symbiotic parent. In contrast, conventional group therapy works with gradually deepening but historically unrelated relationships that bring in a multiplicity of interactions among initially unrelated individuals and their emotionally recreated part-familial contexts. The meaning of here-and-now interactions was broadened considerably with the introduction of conjoint family therapy where the gap between observable interactions and inferred relationships diminishes greatly.

Although the search for conceptual clarification of family therapy is a useful pursuit, it may be premature. Individual-based psychiatric nosology or therapeutic rationale is still far from being universally defined and accepted. Whether family therapy is considered as a derivative of this more conventional approach, or as an elaboration of group therapy, or as a separate and independent method of treatment, its history is too brief to have achieved a firm conceptual framework.

The most frequent question posed to the family therapist by individual therapists concerns the specific areas of indication for a "patient" to be treated with his family. This question is apt to sound inverted to the practitioner of family therapy; for him the value of *any* individual-based psychiatric nosology is limited, even for disorders based on verifiable organic medical conditions. Once nosology is seen in terms of multipersonal interaction patterns, the therapist finds indicational criteria in terms of one family member impractical, restricting, and sometimes even misleading. He is aware that today's seemingly "well" sibling may be discovered to be tomorrow's identified "patient," in reaction to any change in the equilibrium in the family. There is as yet no psychiatric nosology based on multipersonal interaction patterns. Therefore, the family therapist is unable to give a logical and consistent answer to the individual therapist who asks about specific indications. The "mutation" leading from the individual to the relational or contextual concept of disorder may turn out to be as radical a departure in psychiatry as cellular theory was in medicine. The impact of both is long-range and upon basic understanding rather than upon therapeutic techniques per se.

In sociological and small group theory attention is usually confined to the here-and-now, observable characteristics of interacting groups. However, even ad hoc group interactions include the present and past subjective experiences of all members as motivational determinants. In case of a family, the here-and-now of interactional behavior is motivationally inseparable from the family's immediately preceding interactions as well as from the family's past. The relative who lives in the home but doesn't come to the meetings is just as important and active a participant of the total field as those present and observable in the here-and-now. In other words, relational dynamics are more complex than interactional dynamics, if the latter term connotes interactions confined to the observational situation.

The profound difference between the relational context of family therapy on the one hand and of individual or conventional group therapy on the other results in such a conceptual shift that communication of experiences between the two kinds of therapists may be very difficult. For example, what is called "transference distortion" in a patient-therapist or patient-patient intragroup context is the basic climate of intermember relationships within a family. Familial or close relationships involve emotionally determined, wishful reincarnations of past infantile relationships that then are the substances of falling in love, being painfully rejected, being wishfully fused, etc. A main difference is that a parent can be both the former real partner and source of an early, formative relational pattern as well as both target and partner of a current "inappropriate" reenactment of the early pattern; in an "artificial" individual or group therapeutic relationship the pattern is mainly re-enacted in "transference" to the therapist or a co-patient.

Consideration of the differences between interactions in an ad hoc group versus close relationships in a family leads the family therapist to the conceptual problem of defining the "invisible" dimensions of long-term involvements among family members.

Any current interaction in a homeostatically regulated long-term chain of processes is qualified and influenced by the feedback effects of the participants' shared past experiences and future hopes. A rebellious act in a previously subdued child, for instance, has a different meaning from the same behavior in a traditionally boisterous sibling. The child who in the parent's imagination should never truly separate is not resented for the same self-defeating behavior for which the "shining light" of the family would be. On a practical level, the same dimensions cause much of the methodological gap between family therapists and interactional researchers. It is as though, at the present time, without a therapeutic commitment to the long-range process of people's lives, the investigator were prohibited from entering a whole range of behavioral determinants. The point of entry to the "mechanism" of people's lives is, of course, also the point of departure between subjective experience and observable behavior.

The Origins of Family Theory

Family theory, like psychoanalytic theory, originates mainly from efforts to help the disturbed family. Its building stones have been explanatory hypotheses for the purpose of describing and affecting the pathological or pathogenic factors observable and inferable during family therapy of one kind or another. It shares interest with sociology insofar as it seeks to define the characteristics of social systems in a group level. On the other hand, family theory remains close to the level of both long-range and intensive emotional need-gratifications of individuals. The dynamics of emotional needs are an indispensible component of the full understanding of functioning on the family level.

Family theory combines two bodies of knowledge: personality dynamics and multipersonal system dynamics. The thorough integration of these two systems levels into a comprehensive theory is a long-range task. It is not surprising that some proponents of family theory emphasize the transactional or multipersonal level as a replacement for, rather than an addition to, our knowledge about the individual system level or mental organization. The future may see the emergence of ideological battles and, at the extreme, of therapeutic fadism based on the notion of *either-or* rather than synthesis of familial and personal levels of conceptualizing. As has already been indicated, the *either-or* alternatives are presented in detail in Chapter 6.

It is logical to expect, though, the ultimate development of a comprehensive theory of close relationships that will integrate the compatible elements of the two approaches. A relational viewpoint of individual personality dynamics may be one of the means of bridging the theoretical gap between our individual-based heritage and the constantly accruing body of knowledge about multiperson system dynamics. On the one hand, no one can seriously question the validity of the biological individual as being the source and central reference point of experiencing and learning. On the other, no objective observer of families or quasi-families can deny the existence of behavioral patterning originating from formative, close familial relationships.

In order that we arrive at a mature integration and a resulting "elegant" theory of close relationships, both component fields (individual personality dynamics and multipersonal system notions) have to develop conceptually as well as methodologically. An even higher demand is perhaps put on the family theoretician if he is asked to produce a theory of workable clinical practices based on an integrated science of individual *and* relational behavior principles. The interlocking nature of the elements of the two theories can be easily illustrated in a concrete situation, e.g., the often-observed case of one member being "scapegoated" by a family. On the one hand, we can describe the pattern on a suprapersonal level: one member has to be the accuser, another the supporter of the accuser, another the accused one, another the unsuccessful defender, and so on. On the other hand, we can study the determinants of the motivational fit between the needs of individual members and the requirements of the transactional system as a whole. For example, a masochistic constellation in a member's need-configuration may predispose him to the role of the scapegoat.

The Future of Family Theory

In the future the most important field of practical application of family theory may not be family therapy but large-scale social planning and the prevention of.disorders. The emergence of community mental health centers may highlight the gap between individual personality theory and the sociological vantage point in approaching the emotional problems of large sectors of the population. Knowledge obtained from the study and treatment of a large variety of families may provide the relational system point of view without which any social planning may miss its best points of leverage. It is likely, for instance, that the key to an improved system of Aid to Dependent Children lies in understanding the role of the male in the fragmented underprivileged family. Making adequate support of mothers and children dependent upon the absence of the fathers destroys family structure. Ultimately, the full utilization of family process principles will require the integration of knowledge about the dynamic processes of subcultures and conflict among groups in society as a whole.

The questionnaire included three items (VII: 1–3, Appendix 2) directed toward the conceptual framework used by our respondents. In effect, we attempted to ascertain:

1. Whether the respondent used the medical model of health-illness or some other conceptual framework.
2. Whether those using the health-illness framework considered a particular member or the whole family to be "sick."
3. What theoretical position the respondent found useful in family therapy.

A majority of respondents, some 200, reported the use of the medical health-illness model in the family therapy. Among these, there was a clear tendency to view illness as residing in the family and individual member(s) combined. The numbers reporting that they typically view illness as residing only in individual family members were signficantly low.

A smaller number (110) answered the question about theoretical position. Among these "family theory" and "psychodynamic" were by far the most preferred, an indication of the importance of these two foci for family therapists. If the respondents are broken down according to their professional affiliations (See Table 3), psychiatrists and social workers both appear to share these preferences. Psychologists are apparently less polarized, favoring "behavioral," "learning," and "existential" theories to an almost comparable degree.

The meaning of "family theory" is, of course, complex and difficult to define. It seems to connote a dynamic system approach, a link between individual-based personality theory and the more impersonal sociological notions about groups. Furthermore, the term seems to be used to describe collectively the thoughts of pioneering family therapists and conceptualizers.

The responses of the first 127 respondents were analyzed in detail regarding identified theorists in the field of family therapy who had influenced their work. It is interesting to notice the geographical and professional characteristics of this group of respondents. Geographically, they were based in: California, 37 per cent; other points west of the Mississippi, 20 per cent; east of the Mississippi, 39 per cent; no location given, 4 per cent. Their professions were identified as: psychiatrists, 36 per cent; psychologists, 18 per cent; social workers, 35 per cent; others (nurses, pediatricians, M.D.'s, marriage and family counselors, sociologists, etc.), 11 per cent. All authorities cited by at least three respondents are listed in Table 4.

It is apparent from this table that geographical location and professional adherence affect the choice of influential figures in

TABLE 3

Preference for Theoretical Framework According to Respondents' Professions (N = 110)

Theoretical Framework	Psychodynamic A*	U*	S*	N*	Behavioral A	U	S	N	Learning A	U	S	N	Small Group Theory A	U	S	N	Family Theory A	U	S	N	Existential A	U	S	N
Psychiatrists N = 41	10 24%	19 46%	8 19%			6 15%	13 31%	3 7%	1 2%	5 12%	13 31%	4 9%	3 7%	7 16%	12 29%	5 12%	9 22%	23 56%	8 19%	1 2%	6 15%	9 22%	9 22%	
Total who used framework	(37, 90%)				(19, 46%)				(19, 46%)				(22, 53%)				(40, 97%)				(15, 36%)			
Psychologists N = 20	5 25%	4 20%	5 25%		1 5%	3 10%	6 30%		1 5%	4 20%	6 30%			3 10%	4 20%		2 10%	11 50%			1 5%	4 20%	6 30%	
Total who used framework	(14, 70%)				(10, 50%)				(11, 55%)				(7, 35%)				(13, 65%)				(11, 55%)			
Social workers N = 38	13 34%	10 26%	10 26%		4 10%	4 10%	13 34%	1 3%	2 5%	5 13%	12 31%		2 5%	2 5%	12 31%	2 5%	15 40%	14 37%	5 13%		1 3%	7 18%	6 16%	3 8%
Total who used framework	(33, 87%)				(21, 55%)				(19, 50%)				(16, 42%)				(34, 90%)				(14, 37%)			
Others N = 11	3 27%	5 45%	3 27%		2 18%		5 45%				5 45%			2 18%	3 27%		3 27%	6 55%	2 18%			3 27%	1 9%	
Total who used framework	(11, 100%)				(7, 63%)				(5, 45%)				(5, 45%)				(11, 100%)				(3, 27%)			

*"A" = Always "U" = Usually "S" = Sometimes "N" = Never

TABLE 4

Family Therapy Theorists Cited as Influential (N = 127)*

Theorist	To-tal	By Area			By Professional Affiliation			
		Calif.	West	East	Psychi-atrists	Psychol-ogists	Social Work-ers	Oth-ers
Satir	54	32	13	9	15	8	25	6
		59%	24%	17%	27%	14%	48%	11%
Ackerman	52	14	15	23	16	7	25	4
		27%	29%	44%	31%	13%	48%	8%
Jackson	51	27	6	18	21	10	15	5
		53%	12%	35%	41%	20%	29%	10%
Haley	32	13	8	11	11	7	9	5
		41%	25%	34%	34%	22%	28%	16%
Bowen	24	2	4	18	8	4	9	3
		8%	17%	75%	33%	17%	38%	12%
Wynne	19	4	5	10	13	1	4	1
		21%	16%	53%	69%	5%	21%	5%
Bateson	17	5	4	6	7	3	6	1
		29%	23%	35%	41%	18%	35%	6%
Bell	15	7	5	3	5	3	5	2
Boszormenyi-Nagy	9	2	1	6	2	2	4	1
Sullivan	6	3	1	2	2	3	1	
Lidz et al.	6	2	2	2	4	1	1	
Brody	5	1	2	2	2	1	1	1
Spiegel	5			5	3		1	1
Whitaker	5		1	4	2		3	
Kempler	4	4					4	
Paul	4	1	1	2	2	1	1	
MacGregor	3	1	1	1	2			1
Minuchin	3	1		2			1	1
Scheflen	3	1		2		1	1	1
Singer	3	3			3			
Szurek	3	3			2			1

* Percentages are indicated separately by area and professional affiliation only for theorists most frequently mentioned.

the field of family therapy. This suggests the importance of personal availability of a teacher in a particular region as well as his more general influence through published books and articles. Among the 10 most frequently mentioned authorities are six psychiatrists, one social worker, one psychologist, one communications expert, and one cultural anthropologist.

Whatever the ultimate value of the family therapy approach may be historically, it has introduced radically new concepts into the mental health professions. Since, in family therapy, the pathogenic condition is assumed to reside, at least partly, in the multipersonal system of interactions, the traditional medical focus is altered; the theoretical implications of this alteration are bound to be discussed and elaborated for many years. The almost equal preference for family theory and psychodynamic theory among family therapy practitioners indicates the need for an integration of these two frameworks into a comprehensive, balanced framework in which the relationship between the two is clarified. It is conceivable that the psychiatry of the future will be radically altered by a shift from individual to relational psychology as its theoretical understructure.

5

TECHNIQUES AND PRACTICES

When family treatment was first separated out as a special type of therapy, it was generally defined as the treatment of the whole family group in conjoint interviews. This practice, rather than a new theory, distinguished family therapy from other therapeutic procedures. As the field developed and family therapists accumulated experience, family therapy increasingly became a new theoretical orientation toward the psychiatric problem and less a method that can be defined by the number of bodies in the room with the therapist.

Family therapy today is not a treatment method in the usual sense; there is no generally-agreed-upon set of procedures followed by practitioners who consider themselves family therapists. What these practitioners hold in common is the premise that psychopathology in an individual may be an expression of family pathology and the conviction that seeing a family together may offer advantages over seeing its members individually. From these basic views various kinds of therapeutic intervention can emerge, and all of them must be considered family therapy. Some family therapists will interview only the whole family; others will see pairs of individuals as well as the whole group; still others typically see only an individual but with the goal of changing his family context so that he can change.

This chapter will describe some of the techniques and practices now evident in the field. The description is based on conversations with family therapists, observations of their work, and the data generated by the questionnaire.

In the development of the field of family therapy, there has been a widening definition of the family and a concomitant increase in the numbers included in therapeutic sessions. At first, mothers and children were the point of focus; later, fathers were thought to be essential; then, siblings were included; finally, extended kin began to be brought into the picture as their involvement was recognized. For actual treatment sessions, the majority of our respondents prefer the nuclear family of parents and children as the unit, although the therapist may keep in mind their involvement with the extended family. Sixty per cent reported that they sometimes see extended kin; an equal percentage reported that they sometimes focus on the marital pair. Over half the respondents include a significant non-family member. There is a general inclination to include whomever the family considers important to them; as one family therapist remarked, "If there are going to be ghosts in the room, they might as well be there as bodies."

Although the theoretical orientation tends to be toward the whole family unit, the decision about whom to include in treatment sessions is handled flexibly by most therapists. A majority of our respondents reported that they prefer sometimes to see the whole family, sometimes only a few members. Sixty per cent see the family conjointly and also hold individual interviews; an equal number will at times have a member see another therapist. Some family therapists, as a matter of policy, will have a young adult see an individual therapist in the course of family treatment to help ease him out of the family into a life of his own. Among those therapists who prefer to see the whole family together, 78 per cent are willing to relax this policy on clinical grounds. Over 70 per cent hold family sessions even when some family members are absent; apparently they don't handle the "absent-member-maneuver" by canceling the session. It should be clear that the decision made by a therapist in this regard is not whimsical; it may derive from concern about secrets in the family, or from awareness of the absence as a manifestation of resistance at a particular juncture in the course of treatment, or from the felt need to provide support by accepting the absence. As with any tactical decision in the conduct of a family treatment program, a number of complex issues are involved.

In the sequence of treatment sessions, it is possible to see the whole family first and then shift to an individual focus or to do the reverse. These two sequences seem equally popular with our respondents, with 70 per cent reporting that they pursue either one. However, 28 per cent always see the whole family without ever shifting to individuals, as opposed to 10 per cent who see individuals only without ever seeing the whole family. Apparently, one therapist in four prefers to stay with the whole family as the only unit of treatment. Although seeing multiple family units in one group is not a frequent practice, about 15 per cent of our respondents reported having done this.

In respect to the number of therapists at therapeutic sessions, most of our respondents (90 per cent) reported that they usually work alone with the family. Sixty-eight per cent sometimes have two therapists in the room. Only 6 per cent reported the regular use of two therapists. More than half the respondents noted the occasional presence of someone other than another therapist—a student, supervisor, or observer.

Those who consistently or occasionally practice co-therapy have cited various arguments in favor of this arrangement. There is, it is said, so much going on in a family session that two caretakers are required to keep up with the developments. When the co-therapists are male and female (and 60 per cent reported their use of this arrangement), there is the possibility of offering the family a parental model, the therapists behaving as parents should. Other respondents mentioned that, in work with schizophrenics, two therapists were necessary because one might be driven crazy. Still others indicated that with two therapists, one had the freedom to enter into the psychotic system during the session, since another was there to do the administration and pick up the pieces.

In co-therapy, it is common for one of the pair to be a psychiatrist or psychologist, the other a social worker. The majority of respondents involved in co-therapy reported that the two therapists were considered to have equal rank; only 16 per cent described the situation as having one therapist "in charge." Disagreements arising between the therapists are usually acknowledged in the presence of the family, although most respondents work out such altercations outside the treatment room. In this connection, an argument in favor of the single therapist should be mentioned—that it is difficult enough to keep up with what is happening in the family without adding the difficulties of relationships between co-therapists.

Therapists tend to continue the method with which they began to practice family therapy: if they started alone, they continue alone; if they started in co-therapy, they continue in that pattern. Those who typically use two therapists are not necessarily rigid in this arrangement; 20 per cent reported sometimes changing one of the therapists, and 30 per cent reported sometimes shifting to a single therapist. Perhaps in family therapy the co-therapist is seen as a replaceable part in the system.

In respect to the setting for therapeutic sessions, 90 per cent of respondents reported that they usually or always see the family in their offices; only 6 per cent regularly see the family at home. However, a surprisingly high percentage, 70 per cent, occasionally interview the family at home; and over 40 per cent had made a home visit within the previous year. Those who endorse the practice of home visits argue that the family is different on its own territory than in the therapist's office, that one home visit provides more information than a number of office interviews. Despite these alleged advantages, most therapists find regular treatment in the home impractical.

Once a week is the typical frequency of family therapy sessions, with 90 per cent of our respondents reporting this as the usual arrangement. Sometimes the interviews are even less frequent; 70 per cent reported sometimes seeing families less often than weekly. Only 4 per cent of our respondents usually see a family twice a week, although 68 per cent sometimes do. Four-fifths of all respondents never see a family more than twice a week. These frequency figures merit careful consideration. The individual treatment of schizophrenia on this kind of schedule would be thought inadequate, yet it is common for whole families of schizophrenics to be interviewed on a once-a-week schedule.

The rationale for the once-a-week interview is not clear, although three possible explanations can be advanced. The logistic problems of collecting the family for an interview, often in the evening so as not to interfere with the father's working hours, may preclude a more frequent meeting schedule. Perhaps the tolerance limits of therapists restrict the number of meetings. Or it may be that treatment pursued according to this schedule has proved successful.

One is inclined to suspect that either tradition or economics dictates the length of the family treatment session. Although many family therapists claim that it isn't easy to turn off a family as an individual precisely on the minute and that an hour and a half is required to get something started and resolved in a family, 83 per cent of respondents prefer the 50-minute hour. However, over 60 per cent reported sometimes having sessions extending from one to two hours; about a third reported sometimes exceeding two hours. (It is interesting that a third of the respondents reported sometimes seeing a family for less than 50 minutes.)

The impression in the field is that family treatment is typically of briefer duration than individual treatment. The majority of family therapists questioned, however, do not set brief treatment as their goal; they reported a two-to-one preference for long-term treatment, although about half mentioned sometimes attempting either long or short treatment.

Most family therapists seem to be persistent with their families; 71 per cent prefer to see a family regularly until the problems are resolved, while only 8 per cent typically see families with intermittent recesses. Here again, the data indicate some flexibility in practice; 64 per cent reported that they sometimes see families for a short time, then recess, then resume treatment, though 26 per cent reported that they never use this schedule.

A majority of the family therapists questioned (66 per cent) charge the same rate for family sessions as for individual treatment interviews. Eighteen per cent, however, apparently feel that family treatment deserves a higher fee and make their charges accordingly.

Among our respondents, half reported that they introduce drugs into their family treatment, whereas half never do; these figures undoubtedly reflect our mixed sample of medical and non-medical therapists. The introduction of drugs into family treatment is more complex a process than in individual treatment. To give drugs to the "identified patient" firmly labels him as the patient, whereas family therapists usually identify the whole family as the patient. Fifteen per cent of the respondents reported giving drugs only to an identified patient, while 30 per cent reported giving drugs to other family members as well. Those who use drugs generally feel that they facilitate family therapy. A fourth of the total group, however, feel that drugs have no consistent impact and 4 per cent believe that they impede therapy.

It is generally assumed in the field of family therapy that a major part of the therapeutic task consists of lifting the label of patient from one member and allowing the whole family to share that honor. Often, particularly after hospitalization has clearly identified one person as the problem, the family consolidates around the idea that a single person should be the focus of the treatment. Some therapists attempt a frontal assault on this idea by requiring at the outset of treatment that all family members concede that they are patients; of our sample, one-fourth reported doing this, whereas three-fourths reported that they do not. Many prefer to let the process of therapy clarify what unit is to receive the label, and the majority feel that the question of labels is best not made an explicit issue. Even the labeling of treatment itself is often left open: a third of our respondents tell the family it is in therapy; a fourth call it counseling; 10 per cent do not explicitly name the process in dealing with the family.

Many family therapists, particularly those who were trained with a psychoanalytic view, began their practice of family therapy by sitting quietly and making occasional interpretations to families. Most have found this passive stance inadequate in family treatment where the family committing mayhem during the session is apt to interpret the therapist's silence as approval. Most family therapists deem it necessary to intervene actively during family sessions, though their modes of intervention are various.

The majority of respondents prefer to indicate how family members should behave in the session (e.g., express their attitudes and ideas), but give no instructions about behavior outside the treatment room. Only 22 per cent always or usually give instructions for family members to follow outside, although 61 per cent sometimes do. About half of those who give such advice direct family members to behave more rationally, whereas the other half prefer more oblique suggestions designed to induce a change.

Problems in Conducting Family Interviews

The conduct of family interviews presents several problems. Who should discipline children who become unruly, the parents or the therapist? Should the family be permitted to talk freely in any direction or should the therapist control the subject matter in order to achieve particular ends? Should the therapist talk to family members in turn or encourage them to talk to each other? Our data indicate the therapists resolve these problems flexibly. A large majority (90 per cent) prefer to use both methods of eliciting talk from family members, addressing individual members and also encouraging talk within the family. About 60 per cent sometimes control the children and topics that are discussed; 13 per cent always exert this control, and 25 per cent never do. In respect to struggles within the family, 60 per cent of respondents reported sometimes taking sides, but the majority prefer a neutral role and, presumably, typically implement this preference by not taking sides.

It is interesting to compare family therapy with the individual psychodynamic therapy, since many family therapists have been influenced by the latter approach. Characteristically, dynamic treatment includes the therapist's attempt to relate the patient's past to his present, to avoid the expression of his own feelings, and to offer consistent transference interpretations. Among our respondents, the majority attempt to relate the past of the family to its present situation. In respect to the therapist's own expressiveness, however, there is a departure from the usual psychoanalytic approach: 29 per cent typically discuss their own feelings as they are aroused in a session; 60 per cent sometimes do; only 10 per cent never do. In respect to transference, one-third of our respondents reported never discussing transference explicitly; about half sometimes discuss it; and 16 per cent typically do. It appears that interpreting and working through the transference is not a major focus in family treatment.

The discussion of sex in family interviews with children present is also handled flexibly by most respondents. The majority exclude the children when the personal sex life of the parents is discussed but not when sex in general is the topic. Unfortunately, the questionnaire did not inquire whether parents were ex-

cluded during discussions of the children's sex life, a clear possibility in family therapy. Only 1 per cent of respondents
reported never discussing sex at all in the course of therapeutic
sessions with families.

Whereas individual therapy developed largely in a strictly
private setting, family treatment seems to be a much monitored
form of therapy. Family treatment centers are typically equipped
with a one-way mirror arrangement to permit observation.
Among our respondents, 60 per cent reported having observed
the family treatment of other therapists. The majority, however,
do not have their own family therapy observed, since they see
patients in private practice. Twenty-three per cent reported that
their treatment was regularly observed, about 10 per cent for
training purposes. About 40 per cent record their family interviews. Of these, two-thirds use the recordings for group discussions with their peers, and may confront the family with the record of their interactions during interviews. Videotaping is still
rare in the field, with only 12 per cent of respondents reporting
its use.

It is clear that there is not a *method* of family therapy to which
practitioners strictly adhere. Although family therapists have in
common a general orientation, they approach families in a variety
of ways. Family therapy is problem-oriented rather than method-
oriented, and therapists appear to be meeting the needs of the
families they treat with flexible techniques and practices.

6

PREMISES ABOUT FAMILY THERAPY

Between the conceptual framework or theory of family therapy and the techniques of its practices lies a middle ground of operational premises that are either explicitly discussed among therapists or implicit in their work. This area cannot be tapped by questionnaires, nor is the literature in the field, which consists of theoretical statements or detailed case reports, an adequate source of information. It seems useful, therefore, to present some impressions about family therapies gathered from the observation of their work. Perhaps a dozen quite distinct approaches to family treatment can be identified, some of which have been developing for more than 10 years. These approaches were evolved by individuals who began to practice family treatment, often without knowing that others were similarly engaged, and gradually developed their own styles of working with families. Each approach attracted students and followers who in turn attracted students and followers, with the result that several separate "schools" of family therapy are now emerging.

Most family therapists were originally trained in some form of individual therapy, and their theoretical orientations usually reflect their professional background. The psychologist who practices family therapy may emphasize the family as a learning situation; the psychoanalyst can see the family as a dynamic field for developing intrapsychic problems; the family therapist with a social work or communication background will emphasize the communication patterns in family interaction. The debate in the field is about what language to use to describe a family. At a more general level, there is also a debate about how much of the previous language about individuals can be applied when one is attempting to describe and change families. Family therapists tend to polarize on this question. Some see the family as composed of individuals who are describable in the traditional individual terminology. Others argue that a new view of the nature of people has come in with the "discovery" of the family, and that past descriptions of individuals are no longer appropriate because they were made without taking the living context of the person sufficiently into account. Although this distinction is a theoretical one, there are practical consequences in the approach of the therapist to a family. The premises of a family therapist about what to do and how to do it are affected by how much the therapist focuses upon the individual and how much upon the family system.

Approaches to Family Treatment

For purposes of description, the positions closest to the two hypothetical extremes will be compared. *Position A* will locate those one-to-one therapists who occasionally see families but retain a primary focus upon the individual system, and *Position Z* those who use exclusively a family system orientation. One should keep in mind that both positions involve the practice of treating whole families and that, between these two positions, most therapists by far combine these interests in differing proportions. *Position M* might identify those family therapists who see equal validity in an approach to the individual and to the family system, and who may elect to use either or both system levels in conceptualizing about as well as in treating illness. Although the contrasts to be drawn are in great measure caricatures, in that they omit the positions of the greatest number of family therapists who utilize both individual and family system concepts, they may be useful in clarifying the substantive issues introduced into psychiatry by family therapy.

Family therapists in the hypothetic Position A category tend to populate the large academic institutions. They may differ in their background but tend to be in settings where psychoanalysis has great prestige or where conditioning theory of individuals is deeply imbedded. They tend to be therapists who have taken up family therapy while maintaining primary membership in groups devoted to individual therapy. Typically, Position M people are trying to bridge to, or communicate with, colleagues who are continuing to do individual therapy. They argue that the family therapist should have a thorough grounding in individual psychodynamics before approaching family treatment.

A number of family therapists in the Position Z category were formerly psychoanalysts who resigned from that movement; others are psychiatrists, psychologists, or social workers who are not deeply rooted in an academic environment. Still others are from the social sciences with little or no background in individual therapy. Position Z people believe that the family orientation is a discontinuous change from the psychodynamic orientation, and they see the individual focus as a handicap in developing the family system theory they seek.

When family therapists at the extreme positions meet with one another, they agree that one should do family therapy but, except for that common premise, they tend to disagree on many issues. Position A therapists, for example, tend to refer to Position Z therapists as not properly trained; the latter would be likely to say that the former do not grasp the significance of the family system and are not really doing family therapy but treating the individual in the presence of the family.

Illustrations of Differing Premises in the Family Field

Some of the issues upon which the two positions differ can be described to illustrate the differing premises in the family field.

Emphasis on Method vs. Emphasis on Orientation. The Position A family therapists tend to see family therapy more as a

method of treatment—one more procedure in a therapist's repertoire. The Position Z family therapists view it not as a method
but as a new orientation to psychiatry. This conceptual difference
has practical implications. For example, when asked about the
indications and contraindications for family therapy, the Position
A family therapist will attempt to answer the question. The
Position Z family therapist will appear puzzled, since he finds
himself defining any kind of therapy as a way of intervening into
a family. Having shifted his unit of diagnosis and treatment from
the single person to the processes between people, he defines psychopathology as a relationship problem. He cannot say this
person should receive individual therapy and this person family
therapy, because he views individual therapy as one way of intervening into a family. The Position A therapist who treats a
wife will describe himself as dealing with the woman's fantasies,
fears, and hopes; although he would acknowledge that by seeing
the wife and not seeing the husband, he is intervening into a
marriage in a particular way, he would see this process as a uni-
directional sequence in which the change he helps bring about in
the wife in turn brings about change in the marriage. The Position Z therapist might also interview only the wife, but it would
be with an assumption that her problem involves the context in
which she lives and that treatment must both follow from and
result in change in that context. The Position M therapist will
sometimes see his intervention as instrumental in effecting change
directly in the individual patient and indirectly in the marriage,
and at other times he will see his intervention as instrumental in
effecting change directly on the marital relationship.

Identifying the Patient. The Position A therapist, tending to
emphasize the individual patient, views the remainder of the
family as a stress factor. The Position M and Z family therapists
give the family members more equal weight and struggle to find a
better term than "patient" for the family member who is chosen

to be *it*. Terms are used such as "the identified patient" or "the supposed patient" or the "person in pain" or the "person expressing the symptom," and so on. While Position A tends to see a particular individual as a container of psychopathology, Position Z sees the family system as needing some individual to express the pathology of the system. For example, if a child is agitated and is quieted, the mother may become agitated, and if the mother and child are quieted, then the father or a sibling may become agitated because the nature of the system requires it. Therapists in Position M would focus attention both on the individual manifesting the psychopathology and on the family disequilibrium which it betrays. In their view, Position Z therapists fail to recognize that even in a changed interpersonal context the individual patient continues to express the same or similar pathologic behavior.

The Position A therapist tends to see relationships as a product, separate from and external to the patient's intrapsychic life. If a wife is being mistreated by her husband, he will emphasize that the husband is expressing his sadistic aggression and the wife is satisfying her masochistic needs. The Position Z family therapist sees intrapsychic process as caused by the relationship situation. He will describe such a couple as involved in a game in which they must both contribute behavior that keeps their subjective distress continuing. In a similar manner the Position A therapist often sees the child as a victim of the parent's strife or as a scapegoat, while Position Z will view the child as one contributor to, and an essential part of, a continuing sequence of events among all the people involved. The Position M therapist accepts the validity of both individual and interpersonal system dynamics as determinants of pathology.

As a result of this difference, the Position A therapist tends to intervene to get a person to shift his ideas or behavior. The Position Z therapist intervenes to change a sequence of behavior in-

volving several of the people. For example, in an interview a
sequence may be identified as follows: the father will be interro-
gating the child and the child will weakly protest; at a certain
point the mother will come to the support of the child and
attack the father; the father will then back down and apologize.
After a while, the sequence will begin again and repeat itself. The
Position Z family therapist will see the sequence occur and,
when it starts again, he will intervene while the father is interro-
gating the child, just before the mother comes in to attack the
father, or just before the father backs down. His goal is to give
the sequence a different outcome, and he may or may not point
out to the family the nature of the sequence. The Position A
family therapist will tend to see the behavior in smaller units at
any particular moment in therapy, but in a long-range develop-
mental framework, and he will usually intervene to interpret to
the father in order to help him understand why he is behaving
so. He will be thinking about the father's motivations and possibly his history with his own father rather than about the current
sequence of interactions in the family. The Position M therapist
may clarify or interpret either or both the sequence and the
intrapsychic determinants of the individual family members.

The Importance of History. The Position A therapist is typically much more interested in history than is the Position Z
therapist. The former tends to see the family as a collection of
individuals who have introjected their pasts and the therapeutic
problem as lifting the weight of this "programming" out of their
inner space. The Position Z therapist emphasizes the present
situation as the major causal factor and the process that must be
changed. He inquires about the past only when he cannot understand the present or if he thinks the family can discuss the present
more easily if it is framed as something from the past. At times
such a therapist may emphasize the past when he is trying to
define a time when the family members were enjoying each

other more; this is a way of labeling the current problem as a temporary upset as well as clarifying a goal of the therapy. In general, the Position Z family therapist assumes that a current problem must be currently reinforced if it is continuing to exist, while the Position A family therapist assumes that people are responding now to ideas programmed in the past. The Position M therapist believes both assumptions are true, that neither is more true than the other, and that either may offer entry for a therapeutic intervention. He is likely to assume that individuals seek partners with whom they can set up family patterns that repeat and re-enforce in the present their original family patterns.

Diagnosis. Position A tends to put more emphasis upon diagnosing and evaluating the family problem and prefers to gather information before intervening. Such a therapist tends to express diagnostic ideas about the family in the vocabulary of individual therapy, and he prefers to try to define in as much detail as possible the family dynamics. Position Z family therapists tend more readily to accept working with minimal information. Since they tend to place particular emphasis upon the opening session as important to the ultimate therapeutic outcome, because it tends to be a time of family crisis, they wish to intervene as rapidly as possible to take advantage of the opportunity to bring about change. Therefore, they intervene as soon as they have some grasp of what is going on and prefer not to delay therapy for diagnosis and evaluation. Many of them think careful diagnosis serves more to allay the therapist's anxiety than to benefit the family. In conversation such therapists spend much less time talking about differences in family dynamics and more time talking about ways in which they have intervened to bring about changes. Generally, they like to end the first therapy session with some therapeutic aim accomplished so that the family has gained from the encounter and knows what the therapeutic experience will be like. The Position M therapist would fully agree that treatment starts with the first encounter, but he would add that evaluation is a constant element of an ongoing program of treatment.

This more action-oriented point of view does not mean that Position Z therapists only do brief therapy. Often it is long-term, but it is brief when it can be. Position Z therapists emphasize how much can be accomplished with active intervention at a time when a family is in crisis and unstable. They expect that adolescent schizophrenia should be resolved with family treatment at the time of acute onset of the family crisis and not after the adolescent has been hospitalized and the family has stabilized. They argue that, when hospitalization is involved, family treatment can become interminable because each improvement leads to renewed hospitalization. With this view, long-term therapy is seen as necessary to accomplish particular ends rather than as desirable in itself. If the job can be done more quickly, that is done. Typically, they also see change as occurring in discontinuous steps, and they "peg" a change when they get one so that the family continues to the next stage of development and does not slip back. In contrast, Position A family therapists tend to carry over values from individual treatment and to see long-term family therapy as better because it is deeper; at the same time, of course, brief therapy is acknowledged as a valued approach. They see schizophrenia as an individual illness, with the family contributing to it essentially by being a stress factor. They do not consider the hospital as necessarily a handicap in treating the family. The Position M therapist will more frequently be found closer to Position Z than to Position A on this issue.

The Therapist's Role in Diagnosis. A major difference between Position A and Position Z is how much the therapist includes himself in the diagnosis. A Position A therapist describes the family as a set of problems independent of himself, though he is fully aware that they may at any time be responding to his countertransference as well as to his deliberate intervention. The Position Z therapist includes himself in the description of a family. For example, Position A therapists may say "These family members are hostile to each other"; Position Z therapists may say "These family members are showing *me* how hostile they are to each other." This is not a minor distinction. As a consequence, the Position Z therapist does not think of the family as separate from the context of treatment, and he includes himself in that context. He will consider, for example, whether the particular difficulty he sees between a husband and wife is created by the way he is dealing with the couple.

This latter view does not readily allow for different diagnostic categories of families, but instead attempts to describe different families in different treatment contexts, in terms of how the family responds to the intervention of the therapist. An important corollary of this more contextual view is the insistence by Position Z therapists that we must take into account not only the family, including the extended kin who always influence a problem, but also helping professionals who may be involved. To deal with the family, the Position Z therapist argues that he must deal with the wider treatment context, or the total ecological system. The Position A therapist tends to see the wider treatment context or the total ecological system as readily separable from the "real" individual or family problem. This is in no way a denial of the role of the therapist in the doctor-patient interaction, but is an assertion of the independent exisence of a system of pathologic forces and counterforces in the patient.

Since the Position Z therapist tends to think of the patient family as an element in a wider ecological field that includes himself, he is forced to consider that the family's problem may lie in the way he is dealing with the family, and therefore he tends to work more readily toward defining the psychiatric problem in such a way that enables him to bring about change.

The Position A therapist thinks of the family problem as relatively independent of him, and he more readily utilizes the framework of individual therapy, namely, that all he can do is to clarify the problem and try to work with what he finds.

Positive and Negative Affect. A Position A family therapist tends to feel that it is helpful to the family to bring out their underlying feelings openly, no matter what the character of these feelings might be. He interprets to family members how they are responding to each other and expressing their hostility through body movement, and so on. Often he feels this is a way of giving meaning to the behavior of family members. The Position Z family therapist has less enthusiasm for the idea that interpreting feelings and attitudes brings about change. In dealing with hostility between family members, for example, he tends to interpret destructive behavior in some positive way, for example, as a protective act. His premise is that the problem is not to make underlying hostility explicit but to resolve the difficulties in the relationships that are causing the hostility. Therefore, he is more sparse with his interpretations except when using them tactically to persuade family members to behave differently. A Position Z therapist might argue that a Position A therapist seems to be torturing a family by forcing its members to concede their unsavory feelings about each other and that this is a waste of time and not therapeutic. Position A therapists might offer the argument that durable change persists only if the family members express their hostilities and understand why they treat each other as badly as they do, and that Position Z therapists are aiming only for superficial changes in family interaction.

Operational Procedures. Reference was made earlier in this chapter to the fact that a Position A therapist prefers to conceive of family therapy as a method, and tends to define and adhere to a set of procedures with each case. A Position Z therapist tends to feel that any firmly delineated set of procedures is a handicap;

each family is a special problem that may require any one of several different approaches. Instead of fitting the family to a method, the Position Z therapist seeks to devise a way of working that varies with the particular problem presented. Position A family therapists tend more frequently to set rules such as seeing the whole family for a set length of time at set regular intervals. Many Position Z therapists see the whole group to get a total portrait of the situation, but also use other units—a single person, a marital pair, the siblings, or any combination appropriate to the problem. They may see a family regularly or quite irregularly, and they may have a session of several hours at certain points in the conviction that this may save months of more regularly spaced sessions. There is perhaps also a greater willingness to experiment when a particular approach is not working, and they may try out multiple-family therapy and network therapy in which not only the family but friends and neighbors are brought into treatment sessions.

When the Position Z therapist interviews the whole family group together, he puts special emphasis upon getting all the members to participate. If a family member is not speaking, the therapist becomes uncomfortable and tries to involve him. Often he will explicitly turn the family members upon each other so they talk together rather than to him, and when he does this he likes them all to talk. The Position A therapist is more likely to focus upon one person at a time, and tends to have the family members talk to him rather than to each other.

When a therapist intervenes into a family, whether he interviews one person or the whole family group, he is caught up in the struggle of family factions. The Position A therapist, because of his individual focus, tends to avoid siding with some part of the family, and he is particularly prone to side with the child patient against the victimizing parents. In marital struggles he is likely to find himself joining one spouse against another, generally as a response to seeing one as "sicker" than the other. The Position Z family therapist appears to assume flatly that if the therapist sides with one part of a family against another, there will be a poor therapeutic outcome. This is particularly so if he joins one faction while denying he is doing so, which often happens if the therapist still responds to one person as the "patient" but is trying not to. When Position Z therapists take sides, they state this explicitly and announce that they are doing so, usually defining their partisan position as temporary; they are, of course, equally susceptible to taking sides and at the same time denying that they are doing so.

Position M therapists are highly variable with regard to operational procedures and tend to be inconstant within their own practice. They may retain a fairly inflexible set of procedures with one family and be highly flexible with another, depending perhaps on the degree to which they define an individual patient in one instance as generating disturbance in the family and define family disequilibrium in another as generating individual symptoms.

At the most general level, Position A family therapists tend to see the family as a way of gathering additional information about individuals. Position M therapists see family therapy as a qualitative broadening of the scope of theory and practice; in psychiatry by emphasizing both intrapsychic and family dynamics, they add a significant new dimension to individual treatment and a conceptual orientation to psychopathology at a different system level. Position Z family therapists argue that clinicians must share with other behavioral scientists the viewpoint that psychiatric problems are social problems that involve the total ecological system. They prefer to concern themselves with and attempt to change the interlocking systems of the family and the social institutions in which the family is imbedded. Their basic argument is that therapy must develop a new ecological framework for thinking about old problems and that the individual or the family should no longer be fragmented into parts either conceptually or in treatment.

7

ETHICAL ISSUES IN FAMILY TREATMENT

Ethical issues take on a special complexity in the context of family treatment. The psychotherapeutic ethic has, essentially, grown out of the general medical ethic. The welfare of the patient is extolled as paramount, and there are various injunctions against the subversion of this concern, both explicit and implied. When the therapeutic system expands to include family-therapist relationships and the family must be viewed both as an entity and as a collection of constituent individuals, a new formulation of ethical issues is required. How is the family welfare to be defined when family members occupy contending positions? With whom is the therapeutic contract made? To whom is confidentiality owed? In an attempt to attain clarity on these and other issues, we consulted our questionnaire data, the literature on family therapy, and communications from individual practitioners.

It is a central thesis of the present chapter that family therapy directly confronts issues that are present in individual treatment but that can more readily be simplified, camouflaged, or side-stepped in that context. When a patient in individual treatment achieves a change, this change has implications for other people that can be most profound and significant but often is not known to the therapist. Practitioners have long described situations in which a person not in treatment undergoes psychological alteration as a result of the patient's treatment situation. Although the therapist is aware of such possibilities, e.g., marriage, divorce, alterations of homeostatic equilibria, and the like, and is sensitized to their occurrence, he bears no direct responsibility to these significant other persons; his task, therefore, is immeasurably simpler than if one or more of these others were simultaneously in treatment with him. The family therapist must also confront the possibility of decompensation in one family member as another improves. If a shift in familial homeostasis were to occur as a result of individual therapy, say for a son, would the same consequences ensue for his mother? If improvement in one family member were associated with decompensation in another with any frequency, then family treatment would seem to confront more directly the consequences of therapeutic intervention and change than does individual treatment. If different therapeutic routes appear to effect similar results in an individual patient but with different impact upon members of the identified patient's family, then an examination of the alternative treatments on the basis of this consideration becomes necessary. The therapist to begin with will have to consider whether there are equally suitable alternatives; if family treatment turns out to be the only mode offering a reasonable hope of resolving difficulties, he will be prepared to tolerate complications more readily than if individual therapy seems an equally effective route. It is a function of therapeutic skill to be able to assess the degree of stress that each family member will experience in the interaction and his capacity for sustaining it. In treating individuals, a therapist typically makes estimates of a patient's ego strength and pitches the depth and intensity of treatment accordingly. This is not easy in individual treatment, and the difficulties increase exponentially in a family situation.

Family treatment appears to require a redefinition of patient welfare, one that takes into account the minimization of harm and the integration of conflicts between the responsibility the therapist bears to the whole family and his responsibility to its individual members. The newness of family therapy also results in problems of compatibility between research and therapeutic objectives. Rules cannot simply be transferred from individual to family treatment.

Value Conflicts in Family Therapy

Since conflicts or values were thought to be an area in family therapy around which ethical questions might cluster, Items VIII: 1 and 2 in the questionnaire (Appendix 2) were designed to provide information on this topic. Value conflicts can, of course, be especially complicated in family therapy because of the bringing together of the therapist's values not with a single patient's values but with those of a family in which various value systems may be represented. The data generated by these questions are somewhat inconclusive, possibly because some therapists in their practice emphasize family mutuality whereas others see their role as the definition of differences that require accommodation.

An overwhelming majority of family therapists questioned reported value conflicts between family members as occurring frequently or always. A large number also reported occasional conflicts between one family member and the therapist. In respect to the situation where the entire family is in conflict with the therapist, 40 per cent of respondents reported never experiencing this, whereas 57 per cent had observed it sometimes; the same distributions were reported for conflict between the therapist and all but one member of the family. Apparently, therapists observe value conflicts between family members more often than between themselves and all or part of the family. When they do have such conflicts with family members, therapists appear to be most frequently in alliance with the majority of the family.

The responses of family therapists about the nature of value conflicts revealed a wide spectrum of answers. In these conflicts, three major lines of cleavage are discernible: (1) between generations; (2) between a marital pair; (3) between the therapist's value system and that of all or part of the family. There was some blurring of the distinction between differences growing out of symptomatic and character clashes and those clearly ascribable to value differences. It would appear that, on the interpersonal level in the family setting, all differences become value-connected in the sense of reflecting on the participants' self-concepts in relationship to others in the family and to the family as a whole. The problem may not be differences as such but the lack of clearly definable mutualizing factors that makes differences so crucial. Some political theory has it that governments do not get overthrown; they cease to be able to govern when the ever-present centrifugal social forces lose the counterpoise that balances them and the society disintegrates. Families may also lose this balance so that value clashes become more stark and divisive.

Many therapists reported value clashes between dogmatic hierarchical family systems and individuals striving for greater autonomy. In some families, the implicit definition of family needs seems diametrically opposed to the unfolding autonomy of individuals. It appears that most therapists confronted with this kind of conflict exert their influence on the side of individuation and, consonant with their own value systems, seek to soften and modify rigid attitudes. This situation becomes more complicated in issues involving parental expectations of children where the question of autonomy is masked by a parental insistence on academic achievement; conformance with parental expectation appears in the guise of a means towards future autonomy, although it may actually diminish the autonomy of the child.

Some therapists reported clashes emanating from the attempts of families to transmit social mores, usually constraints, to their children. Failures of transmission were manifested in antisocial behavior by the children. In such situations, therapists frequently see their own role as pointing out familial inconsistencies and double messages that may be abetting the acting out. Other therapists provide models of limit setting.

Symbiotic emotional dependency growing out of the needs of parents to keep their children close may become translated into value conflicts about the appropriate character of relationships between family members. The therapist's values generally exert an influence in the direction of loosening this kind of emotional tie, sometimes with the consequence of a serious disruption in the stability of another family member.

Differences between marital partners are expressed in varying conceptions of their respective roles. There is a merging of problems traditionally described from the intrapsychic and interpersonal points of view; sexual problems, for example, grade into those of mutual expectations, self-concepts, affective expression, intellectual styles and interactions. Extramarital activity was frequently cited as a problem in which several of such issues become crystallized.

Therapists frequently encounter families where a positive value is placed on the control of affects and the minimization of their expression; usually they seek to deactivate such positively charged stances. Therapists find that their attempts to counteract or reverse defenses operative in the family such as denial, protection, and isolation are met with the institutionalization of such values as appropriate family modes of relating. Breaking down a family-syntonic mode of functioning involves a value choice. Although individual members may be aided by such a breakdown, there is always a risk that other family members may not do as well as in the old modality. The therapist needs to examine critically the temptation to take sides in order to protect a weaker family member and to prevent scapegoating, to break up mutual dissociation patterns and pseudomutual structures, to undercut medical models in which designated family members are labeled as sick.

Therapists can describe their function in these situations as that of identifying difficulties, of presiding over the exposition of such difficulties, and of achieving homeostasis through family interaction. In reality, family therapists upset homeostatic equilibrium and intervene with values that, for better or for worse, play a part in changes within the family. To recapitulate, these values seem to be: (1) that autonomy is preferable to continuing hierarchical subordination; (2) that self-realization is valuable along with family integrity and stability; (3) that marital relationships are not absolute ends in themselves but must be viewed relative to other considerations; (4) that affective expression and emotional closeness are better than their opposites.

Secrets and Confidentiality

Another area where ethical considerations are important is that relating to confidentiality and the handling of secrets. In individual psychotherapy, the patient's right to privacy is explicitly recognized. It is assumed the entire procedure is focused upon the needs of the patient, and that familial, societal, or therapist needs are subordinate. Privacy and confidentiality are essentials in a system where feelings of shame, anxiety, fear and guilt are counteracted in order to maximize a patient's openness and disclosures. The patient's trust of the therapist is intrinsic to the system.

In family therapy, the situation is more complicated. The trusting relationship built up between therapist and family is not a monolithic entity. Individuals within the family have varying capacities for trust and respond differently to the therapist's capacity for creating such an atmosphere. Among themselves, family members have varying degrees of openness and inwardness, of trust and distrust. In some areas, an entire family may withhold or suppress information.

The problem is in part shaped by the therapist's arrangements for meetings. Obviously, seeing individuals or parts of families alone offers the opportunity for revelations that might not be forthcoming in a meeting with the whole family. Therapists who facilitate such confidence by less-than-whole-family meetings may

diverge in their handling of the information these can provide.
Some therapists view the degree and quality of intrafamilial
communication as a central difficulty in pathological families.
From this point of view, family secrets would seem symptomatic
of the trouble the family is in. The presence of unshared or partially shared secrets is a threat to the family system, and the
main order of therapy is focused on this problem, which is made
the paradigm of the family's troubles. Such therapists often announce at the onset of treatment that they will not keep secrets.
Communications made by a family member after such an an-
nouncement, ostensibly in confidence, are viewed by the therapist
as really intended for transmission. The therapist sees himself
as a communications facilitator, as a link, and invites family
members to use him in this way. In some of our questionnaire
responses, the occurrence of secrets and their withholding was
related to affective blocking and impoverishment of emotional
exchange.

Another group of therapists seems to be involved with pre-
venting the mushrooming of covert alliances and splits as family
therapy proceeds. They announce that they will hear no confidences that cannot be shared with other family members, and
they firmly maintain this position. This group possibly sees
acting out as an important issue and therefore feels inclined to
employ firmness and to set limits. This attitude toward secrets
may also relate to a therapist's differing stance vis-à-vis the
problems and how to handle them. In contrast to his colleagues
in the first group, his is a more directive mode; whereas a
therapist of the first group accepts a family's tendency to split
into factions and to have secrets and accepts their confidences
as grist to the therapeutic mill, a therapist of the second group
labors to prevent these things from happening at all.

A third group makes no prior stipulations and accepts confidences, then proceeds covertly and overtly to get the bearer to

reveal the confidence himself or to give the therapist permission to reveal it. Thus confidence is ostensibly kept and the ethical criteria met, while at the same time pressures are exerted toward therapeutic goals. Some therapists focus on such issues intensively, whereas others treat them along with many comparable issues that might emerge in family transactions.

Still another group accepts individual confidences, indeed often encourages them, and keeps such items isolated from the mainstream of family therapeutic activity. With the aim of maintaining individual trust relationships while building family relations, therapists of this group attempt a syncretic amalgam of individual confidence modes with the family therapy system. These therapists place great importance upon their individual relationships with family members. How this affects their relationship to the family as an entity is an open question. In general, therapists of this group define a normative family system as one in which individual secrets or two-person confidences can exist without decisively impairing the stability of the whole family system. Stated another way, they see a greater threat to family homeostasis and function in the complete abrogation of barriers than in their being maintained. Many of these therapists, in addition to conjoint family interviews, see family members individually, and fuse individual and family treatment.

There are many therapists who approach secrets and confidentiality by assessing some secrets as better kept than not. Secrets that are judged to threaten family homeostasis if revealed (e.g, marital infidelity) are considered worth keeping. Sometimes a therapist participates in a protective confidentiality with a specific family member who seems particularly marked or damaged by family interaction; this person is seen as requiring special handling in order to foster his capacities for trust, to diminish his vulnerability to other family members, and to increase his autonomy and undercut his symbiotic dependence.

Privileged Communication

Closely related to the issue of confidentiality and secrecy among family members is the legal issue of privileged communication. Can one member of the family later ask the therapist to testify against another member of the family? Is the permission of all required before the therapist releases information to those outside of the family? This question is particularly important in situations that go on to divorce. In some of those instances family therapists have been asked to testify.

Most therapists feel that confidentiality within the family is important and that information coming out in the family therapy should not be used in subsequent legal actions. The situation is complicated in family therapy because most legal rules about privilege relate to a single patient or client relating to a single therapist. The presence of a third person is usually taken to mean waiver of the privilege.

There are some beginning developments, however, suggesting that a privilege for the family can be established. First, in those states that now have or in which it is proposed to establish conciliation procedures prior to divorce litigation, information revealed during conciliation or counseling efforts is considered privileged. Second, isolated cases have been reported in which the counselor has claimed that the information could not be released without the consent of both parties, and this position has been accepted by the court.

If the principle of privilege is to be developed, family therapists will have to take the consistent position that it is unethical to release information without the consent of the family, even to the point of risking citations for contempt of court.

It will probably prove simpler for family therapists to work out ethical standards that encompass particular questions of competence, values, and the treatment of confidences than it will to make more general decisions about the matrix that nurtures all these issues. A family is a dynamic synthesis of antagonistic as well as mutualizing forces. How is serving "the good of all family members" to be interpreted, and how is that interpretation to be effectively implemented?

The good of the family unit may be difficult to define in practice. There may be irreconcilable differences between its members. The family unit's existence as an entity in no wise negates the existence of individual members with characteristics and interests that cannot necessarily be dealt with via the whole family. Individuation and identity may grow out of opposition between family members, or the family may be strengthened by the capacity to integrate these opposing forces. We need to clarify generally and in specific applications what those family interests are that are to be benefited, and how they are to be viewed when they clash with the interests of individual members. There is no assurance that this need can be readily satisfied. As in the larger society, there are those who view dissent as debilitating, whereas others see it as meaningful and necessary to viability and progress. Perhaps the most that family therapists can hope for is careful attention to these ethical issues rather than the attainment of hard-and-fast answers.

EPILOGUE

It has been our purpose to report on the present state of the field of family therapy. It is clear enough that in a field so new and so rapidly changing, one cannot confidently go beyond the identification and rather general description of some of the ideas and practices shaping the art of family therapy. As experience accumulates, a more solid body of knowledge may develop. Meanwhile, it seems useful to underscore some of the salient observations in this report.

As has already been emphasized, the most striking characteristic of family therapy at this time is the tendency of therapists to cluster into two groups—those who view the family as a complicating factor in any individual member's intrapsychic struggles and those who view the transactions of the family as determining, in a dynamic way, the responses and attitudes of its members. Perhaps such polarization will increase, but it seems more likely that family therapy will evolve concepts that combine these points of view in a new and broader ideology. There would, it appears, be some gain if therapists who treat individual patients were to enlarge their scope of interests to include the whole family and to focus their treatment attention somewhat more evenly upon its various members, in the manner of the transactional therapists. Conversely, there would be some gain if transactional practitioners were to assign to history and past experience some of the importance that analytically oriented therapists have always recognized. Indeed, it seems evident that some therapists have already evolved such a compromise in their own practices, and this seems to promise an enrichment of family methods in the future. At the same time, the possibility must be kept open that the shift from the individual to the family is discontinuous and that the effort to develop a middle group is nothing more than an attempt to hold on to the familiar.

We wish to call attention to one impact that the introduction of family therapy has had upon the mental health professions, the consequences of which may be profound. When the unit of diagnosis and treatment shifts from the individual to the family in an agency or institution, there is a consequent shift in the relationships of staff members dealing with patients. The separate disciplines of psychiatry, psychology, social work, and nursing traditionally deal with fairly separate aspects of the problems defined in the treatment of individual patients. In a child guidance clinic, for example, the child psychiatrist generally deals with the child, the social worker interviews the parents, the psychologist tests the child, and if the child is institutionalized the psychiatric nurse manages the ward. This is of course a highly idealized description of a differentiation that perhaps has never been really practiced in pure form, and undoubtedly many forces implicit in community psychiatry programs operate to blur the functional boundaries between disciplines. It is strikingly apparent that family therapy is one such force; when agencies begin to treat the whole family as a unit the differences between the disciplines immediately become obscured. If the psychiatrist treats the whole family and the social worker treats the whole family and the psychologist treats the whole family, what are the functional differences between them? To complicate the matter further, in at least two programs nurses are being trained in family therapy so that the functions of the nurse too will be less differentiated from those of the other professional groups. As the family therapy movement grows, additional pressure may be expected toward eliminating traditional functional differences between the disciplines.

This report points up the obvious need to intensify research efforts in the field of family therapy so that practice can be based more firmly in theory. Eventually, it may be possible to design controlled experiments that permit the study of comparable families under various treatments, although the diversity of personal experiences and perceptions of experience will always make controls at best approximate. Pending the design of sophisticated experiments in the future, it is possible now to accumulate data in forms that will later prove useful. It is not too early, for example, to make earnest efforts toward evolving a common vocabulary for family therapists. Undoubtedly, much of the diversity of language is a reflection of deep-seated differences in how family behavior is conceptualized; but some terms are already in general use and are understood throughout the field, and communication among practitioners as well as the collection of more uniform data would be furthered through a glossary of terms adopted or devised to describe family transactions and the relationship of such transactions to intrapsychic tensions. The time also seems ripe for attention to uniform recording of data so that the raw material that practice generates will be in usable form for future research efforts. Undoubtedly the computer will become the repository for the storage and retrieval of family data. Perhaps a program designer should now be brought in to work with family therapists in developing those data-collecting schedules that are likely to prove the most appropriate. It would be useful if a start were made toward setting up a bank of family histories that include not only past events and treatment but also noninterventional follow-up information.

These are not easy tasks, but they are at least specific and can be approached rather directly. Less amenable to prompt attention are some considerations that underlie the whole area of family therapy. It is assumed that most family therapists have a commitment to the family as a social unit. Is this commitment based on the conviction that the family is a "good" thing, that the family is the most useful satisfying social arrangement that can be envisioned? Or is the commitment a more pragmatic one, based on the recognition that the family is what exists and might as well be helped to function as successfully as possible? Is the viability of the family decreasing? If it is, should the field explore the application of family therapy experience to another kind of unit, or should it work toward reversing the trend? What characteristics have family therapists themselves in respect to their own family problems, and what personal attitudes and experiences have influenced their interest in the field?

At the moment, the challenges to family therapy are numerous. In the field of education, there is an increasing shift to the student-in-the-family as the unit to which the school must direct its attention. In the field of medicine, there is an increasing shift to the patient-in-the-family as the unit to which the school must direct its attention. No longer are schools and medical facilities content to process individuals without any consideration of the family contexts in which they have developed. The information that family therapists acquire about the nature and the effects of such contexts will undoubtedly become vitally useful to those who educate and those who carry on the general practice of medicine.

Indeed, the body of knowledge that family therapists are in the process of accruing may prove even more broadly useful. One may view family problems as, in effect, struggles that center around the sharing of power and responsibility among family members. These are the problems that family therapists seek to resolve, bringing the various members of families into a more comfortable equilibrium with each other. The sharing of power and responsibility is, however, also at the root of intergenerational, interracial, and international problems. Although it is a long-range hope, it may be that what can be learned about restoring or creating equilibrium within the family can be extrapolated to larger system levels—to the university, the city, the society of a nation, and the community of nations.

Appendix I

BIBLIOGRAPHY OF MARRIAGE AND FAMILY THERAPY

1. Ackerman, N. W.: THE PSYCHODYNAMICS OF FAMILY LIFE, Basic Books, Inc., New York, 1958.

2. ————: "Toward an Integrative Therapy of the Family," *American Journal of Psychiatry*, 114:727–733, 1958.

3. ————: "Family Focussed Therapy of Schizophrenia," in THE OUT-PATIENT TREATMENT OF SCHIZOPHRENIA, S. C. Scher and H. R. Davis, eds., Grune & Stratton, Inc., New York, 1960.

4. ————: "A Dynamic Frame for the Clinical Approach to Family Conflict," in EXPLORING THE BASE FOR FAMILY THERAPY, N. W. Ackerman, F. L. Beatman, and S. N. Sherman, eds., Family Service Association of America, New York, 1961.

5. ————: "Emergence of Family Psychotherapy on the Present Scene," in CONTEMPORARY PSYCHOTHERAPIES, The Free Press, Glencoe, Ill., 1961.

6. ————: "Family Psychotherapy and Psychoanalysis: Implications of Difference," *Family Process*, 1:30–43, 1962.

7. ————: TREATING THE TROUBLED FAMILY, Basic Books, Inc., New York, 1966.

8. ————: "Family Psychotherapy Today: Some Areas of Controversy," *Comprehensive Psychiatry*, 7:375–388, 1966.

9. ————: "Family Psychotherapy—Theory and Practice," *American Journal of Psychotherapy*, 20:405–414, 1966.

10. Ackerman, N. W., and Behrens, M. L.: "The Family Group and Family Therapy," in PSYCHOTHERAPY: THE PRACTICAL APPLICATION OF EARLY DIAGNOSIS, Vol. 3, J. H. Masserman and J. L. Moreno, eds., Grune & Stratton, Inc., New York, 1959.

11. Alexander, I. G.: "Family Therapy," *Marriage and Family Living,* 25:146–154, 1963.

12. Alger, I., and Hogan, P.: "The Use of Videotape Recordings in Conjoint Marital Therapy," *American Journal of Psychiatry,* 123:1425–1430, 1967.

13. Appel, E.; Goodwin, H. M.; Wood, H. P.; and Askren, E. L.: "Training in Psychotherapy: the Use of Marriage Counseling in a University Teaching Clinic," *American Journal of Psychiatry,* 117:709–711, 1961.

14. Arlen, M. S.: "Conjoint Therapy and the Corrective Emotional Experience," *Family Process,* 5:91–104, 1966.

15. Arnold, A.: "The Implications of Two-Person and Three-Person Relationships for Family Psychotherapy," *Journal of Health and Human Behavior,* 3:94–97, 1962.

16. Augenbraun, B.; Reid, H. L.; and Friedman, D. S.: "Brief Intervention as a Preventive Force in Disorders of Early Childhood," *American Journal of Orthopsychiatry,* 37:697–702, 1967.

17. Bannister, K., and Pincus, L.: Shared Phantasy in Marital Problems: Therapy in a Four-Person Relationship, Tavistock Institute of Human Relations, London, 1965, 77 pp.

18. Barcai, A. "An Adventure in Multiple Family Therapy," *Family Process,* 6:185–192, 1967.

19. Bardill, D.: "Family Therapy in an Army Mental Hygiene Clinic," *Social Casework,* 44:452–457, 1963.

20. Basamania, B. W.: "The Emotional Life of the Family: Inferences for Social Casework," *American Journal of Orthopsychiatry,* 31:74–86, 1961.

21. Bateson, G.; Jackson, D. D.; Haley, J.; and Weakland, J. H.: "Toward a Theory of Schizophrenia," *Behavioral Science,* 1:251–264, 1956.

22. Beatman, F. L.: "The Training and Preparation of Workers for Family-Group Treatment," *Social Casework,* 45:202–208, 1964.

23. Becker, I.: "Good Premorbid Schizophrenic Wives and Their Husbands," *Family Process,* 2:34–51, 1963.

24. Beecher, W., and Beecher, M.: "Re-Structuring Mistaken Family Relationships," *Journal of Individual Psychology,* 13: 176–181, 1957.

25. Bell, J. E.: FAMILY GROUP THERAPY, Public Health Monograph No. 64, U. S. Department of Health, Education, and Welfare, Washington, D. C., 1961.

26. ———: "Recent Advances in Family Group Therapy," *Journal of Child Psychology and Psychiatry,* 3:1–15, 1962.

27. ———: "A Theoretical Position for Family Group Therapy," *Family Process,* 2:1–14, 1963.

28. ———: "The Family Group Therapist: An Agent of Change," *International Journal of Group Psychotherapy,* 14:72–83, 1964.

29. ———: "Contrasting Approaches in Marital Counseling," *Family Process,* 6:16–26, 1967.

30. Belmont, L. P., and Jasnow, A.: "The Utilization of Co-therapists and of Group Therapy Techniques in a Family Oriented Approach to a Disturbed Child," *International Journal of Group Psychotherapy,* 11:319–328, 1961.

31. Berman, G.: "Communication of Affect in Family Therapy," *Archives of General Psychiatry,* 17:154–158, 1967.

32. Blinder, M. G.; Colman, A. D.; Curry, A. E.; and Kessler, D. R.: "MCFT: Simultaneous Treatment of Several Families," *American Journal of Psychotherapy,* 19:559–569, 1965.

33. Boszormenyi-Nagy, I., and Framo, J. L., eds.: INTENSIVE FAMILY THERAPY: THEORETICAL AND PRACTICAL ASPECTS, Harper & Row, New York, 1965.

34. Boszormenyi-Nagy, I.: "The Concept of Change in Conjoint Family Therapy," in PSYCHOTHERAPY FOR THE WHOLE FAMILY, A. S. Friedman, et al., Springer Publishing Co., Inc., New York, 1965.

35. ———: "Intensive Family Therapy as Process," in INTENSIVE FAMILY THERAPY: THEORETICAL AND PRACTICAL ASPECTS, I.

Boszormenyi-Nagy and J. L. Framo, eds., Harper & Row, New York, 1965.

36. ———: "From Family Therapy to a Psychology of Relationships: Fictions of the Individual and Fiction of the Family," *Comprehensive Psychiatry,* 7:408–423, 1966.

37. Boverman, M., and Adams, J. R.: "Collaboration of Psychiatrist and Clergyman: A Case Report," *Family Process,* 3:251–272, 1964.

38. Bowen, M.: "Family Psychotherapy," *American Journal of Orthopsychiatry,* 31:40–60, 1961.

39. ———: "Family Psychotherapy with Schizophrenia in the Hospital and in Private Practice," in INTENSIVE FAMILY THERAPY: THEORETICAL AND PRACTICAL ASPECTS, I. Boszormenyi-Nagy and J. L. Framo, eds., Harper & Row, New York, 1965.

40. ———: "The Use of Family Theory in Clinical Practice," *Comprehensive Psychiatry,* 7:345–374, 1966.

41. Brodey, W. M.: "The Family as the Unit of Study and Treatment: Image, Object and Narcissistic Relationships," *American Journal of Orthopsychiatry,* 31:69–73, 1961.

42. Brodey, W. M., and Hayden, M.: "The Intrateam Reactions: Their Relation to the Conflicts of the Family in Treatment," *American Journal of Orthopsychiatry,* 27:340–355, 1957.

43. Brody, S.: "Simultaneous Psychotherapy of Married Couples," in CURRENT PSYCHIATRIC THERAPIES, Vol. 1, J. H. Masserman, ed., Grune & Stratton, Inc., New York, 1961.

44. Burks, H., and Serrano, A.: "The Use of Family Therapy and Brief Hospitalization," *Diseases of the Nervous System,* 26:804–806, 1965.

45. Carek, D. J., and Watson, A. S.: "Treatment of a Family Involved in Fratricide," *Archives of General Psychiatry,* 11:533–543, 1964.

46. Carroll, E. J.: "Family Therapy—Some Observations and Comparisons," *Family Process,* 3:178–185, 1964.

47. ———: "Treatment of the Family as a Unit," *Pennsylvania Medical Journal,* 63:56–62, 1960.

48. Carroll, E. J.; Cambor, C. G.; Leopold, J. V.; Miller, M. D.; and Reis, W. J.: "Psychotherapy of Marital Couples," *Family Process,* 2:25–33, 1963.

49. Charney, I. W.: "Family Interviews in Redefining a 'Sick' Child's Role in the Family Problem," *Psychological Reports,* 10:577–578, 1962.

50. Clower, C. G., and Brody, L.: "Conjoint Family Therapy in Outpatient Practice," *American Journal of Psychotherapy,* 18:670–677, 1964.

51. Cohen, I. M., ed.: FAMILY STRUCTURE, DYNAMICS AND THERAPY, Psychiatric Research Report No. 20, American Psychiatric Association, Washington, D.C., January, 1966.

52. Cooper, S.: "New Trends in Work with Parents: Progress or Change," *Social Casework,* 42:342–347, 1961.

53. Coughlin, F., and Wimberger, H. C.: "Group Family Therapy," *Family Process,* 7:37–50, 1967.

54. Curry, A. E.: "Therapeutic Management of Multiple Family Groups," *International Journal of Group Psychotherapy,* 15:90–96, 1965.

55. Cutter, A. V., and Hallowitz, D.: "Diagnosis and Treatment of the Family Unit with Respect to the Character-Disordered Youngster," *Journal of the American Academy of Child Psychiatry,* 1:605–618, 1962.

56. ———: "Different Approaches to Treatment of the Child and the Parents," *American Journal of Orthopsychiatry,* 32:152–158, 1962.

57. Davies, Q.; Ellenson, G.; and Young, R.: "Therapy with a Group of Families in a Psychiatric Day Center," *American Journal of Orthopsychiatry,* 36:134–147, 1966.

58. Dicks, H. V.: MARITAL TENSIONS: CLINICAL STUDIES TOWARD A PSYCHOLOGICAL THEORY OF INTERACTION, Basic Books, Inc., New York, 1967.

59. Elkin, M, "Short-Contact Counseling in a Conciliation Court," *Social Casework,* 43:184–190, 1962.

60. Erickson, M.: "The Identification of a Secure Reality," *Family Process,* 1:294–303, 1962.

61. Feldman, M. J.: "Privacy and Conjoint Family Therapy," *Family Process,* 6:1–9, 1967.

62. Fisch, R.: "Home Visits in a Private Psychiatric Practice," *Family Process,* 3:114–126, 1964.

63. Fisher, S., and Mendell, D.: "The Communication of Neurotic Patterns Over Two and Three Generations," *Psychiatry,* 19:41–46, 1956.

64. Fleck, S.: "Psychotherapy of Families of Hospitalized Patients," in CURRENT PSYCHIATRIC THERAPIES, Vol. 3, J. H. Masserman, ed., Grune & Stratton, Inc., New York, 1963.

65. Fox, R. E.: "The Effect of Psychotherapy on the Spouse," *Family Process,* 7:7–16, 1967.

66. Framo, J. L.: "The Theory of the Technique of Family Treatment of Schizophrenia," *Family Process,* 1:119–131, 1962.

67. ———: "Rationale and Techniques of Intensive Family Therapy," in INTENSIVE FAMILY THERAPY: THEORETICAL AND PRACTICAL ASPECTS, I. Boszormenyi-Nagy and J. L. Framo, eds., Harper & Row, New York, 1965.

68. Freeman, V. J.: "Differentiation of 'Unity' Family Therapy Approaches Prominent in the United States," *International Journal of Social Psychiatry,* Special Edition 2, 35–46, 1964.

69. ———: Klein, A. F.; Riehman, L. M.; Lukoff, I. F.; and Heisey, V. E.: " 'Family Group Counseling' as Differentiated from Other Family Therapies," *International Journal of Group Psychotherapy,* 13:167–175, 1963

70. Friedman, A. S.: "Family Therapy as Conducted in the Home," *Family Process,* 1:132–140, 1962.

71. ———: "The Incomplete Family in Family Therapy," *Family Process,* 2:288–301, 1963.

72. ———: "The 'Well' Sibling in the 'Sick' Family: A Contradiction," *International Journal of Social Psychiatry,* Special Edition 2, 47–53, 1964.

73. Fry, W. F.: "The Marital Context of an Anxiety Syndrome," *Family Process,* 1:245–252, 1962.

74. Gehrke, S., and Kirschenbaum, M.: "Survival Patterns in Family Conjoint Therapy," *Family Process,* 6:67–80, 1967.

75. Gehrke, S., and Moxom, J.: "Diagnostic Classifications and Treatment Techniques in Marriage Counseling," *Family Process,* 1:253–264, 1962.

76. Geist, J., and Gerber, N. M.: "Joint Interviewing: A Treatment Technique with Marital Partners," *Social Casework,* 41:76–83, 1960.

77. Glasser, Paul H.: "Changes in Family Equilibrium During Psychopathology," *Family Process,* 2:245–264, 1963.

78. Goodwin, H., and Mudd, E.: "Indications for Marriage Counseling: Methods and Goals," *Comprehensive Psychiatry,* 7:450–461, 1966.

79. Goolishian, H. A.: "A Brief Psychotherapy Program for Disturbed Adolescents," *American Journal of Orthopsychiatry,* 32:142–148, 1962.

80. ————: McDonald, E. G.; MacGregor, R.; Ritchie, A. M.; Serrano, A. C.; and Schuster, F. P.: MULTIPLE IMPACT THERAPY WITH FAMILIES, McGraw-Hill Book Co., New York, 1961.

81. Gralnick, A.: "The Family in Psychotherapy," in SCIENCE AND PSYCHOANALYSIS, Vol. 2, INDIVIDUAL AND FAMILY DYNAMICS, J. H. Masserman, ed., Grune & Stratton, Inc., New York, 1959.

82. ————: "Family Psychotherapy: General and Specific Considerations," *American Journal of Orthopsychiatry,* 32:515–526, 1962.

83. ————: "Conjoint Family Therapy: Its Role in Rehabilitation of the Inpatient and Family," *Journal of Nervous and Mental Disease,* 136:500–506, 1963.

84. Green, R.: "Collaborative and Conjoint Therapy Combined," *Family Process,* 3:80–98, 1964.

85. Greenberg, L. M.; Glick, I. D.; Match, S.; and Riback, S. S.: "Family Therapy: Indications and Rationale," *Archives of General Psychiatry,* 10:7–25, 1964.

86. Grosser, G. H., and Paul, N. L.: "Ethical Issues in Family Group Therapy," *American Journal of Orthopsychiatry*, 34: 875–884, 1964.

87. Gurney, B., and Gurney, L. F.: "Choices in Initiating Family Therapy," *Psychotherapy*, 1:119–123, 1964.

88. Gullerud, E. N., and Harlan, V. L.: "Four-Way Joint Interviewing in Marital Counseling," *Social Casework*, 43:532–537, 1962.

89. Haley, J.: "Whither Family Therapy," *Family Process*, 1:69–100, 1962.

90. ————: "Marriage Therapy," *Archives of General Psychiatry*, 8:213–234, 1963.

91. ————: STRATEGIES OF PSYCHOTHERAPY, Grune & Stratton, Inc., New York, 1963.

92. Haley, J., and Hoffman, L.: TECHNIQUES OF FAMILY THERAPY, Basic Books, Inc., New York, 1967.

93. Hallowitz, D.; Clement, R. G.; and Cutter, A. V.: "The Treatment Process with Both Parents Together," *American Journal of Orthopsychiatry*, 27:587–601, 1957.

94. Hallowitz, D., and Cutter, A. V.: "The Family Unit Approach in Therapy: Uses, Process and Dynamics," CASEWORK PAPERS, Family Service Association of America, New York, 1961.

95. Hallowitz, D.: "Family Unit Treatment of Character-Disordered Youngsters," in SOCIAL WORK PRACTICE, Columbia University Press, New York, 1963.

96. Handel, G., ed.: THE PSYCHOSOCIAL INTERIOR OF FAMILY LIFE, Aldine Publishing Co., Chicago, 1967.

97. Handlon, J. H., and Parloff, M. B.: "The Treatment of Patient and Family as a Group: Is It Group Psychotherapy?" *International Journal of Group Psychotherapy*, 12:132–141, 1962.

98. Hansen, C.: "An Extended Home Visit with Conjoint Family Therapy," *Family Process*, 7:67–87, 1967.

99. Harms, E.: "A Socio-Genetic Concept of Family Therapy," *Acta Psycotherapica*, 12:53–60, 1964.

100. Hoffman, L., and Kantor, R. E.: "Brechtian Theater as a Model for Conjoint Family Therapy," *Family Process,* 5:218–229, 1966.

101. Jackson, D. D.: "Schizophrenic Symptoms and Family Interaction," *Archives of General Psychiatry,* 1:618–621, 1959.

102. ————: "Family Interaction, Family Homeostasis, and Some Implications for Conjoint Family Psychotherapy," in SCIENCE AND PSYCHOANALYSIS, Vol. 2: INDIVIDUAL AND FAMILIAL DYNAMICS, J. H. Masserman, ed., Grune & Stratton, Inc., New York, 1959.

103. Jackson, D. D., and Weakland, J. H.: "Conjoint Family Therapy: Some Considerations on Theory, Technique and Results," *Psychiatry,* 24:30–45, 1961.

104. Jackson, D. D., and Satir, V.: "A Review of Psychiatric Developments in Family Diagnosis and Family Therapy," in EXPLORING THE BASE FOR FAMILY THERAPY, N. W. Ackerman, F. L. Beatman, and S. N. Sherman, eds., Family Service Association of America, New York, 1961.

105. Jolesch, M.: "Casework Treatment of Young Married Couples," *Social Casework,* 43:245–251, 1962.

106. Jones, W.: "The Villain and the Victim: Group Therapy for Married Couples," *American Journal of Psychiatry,* 124:351–354, 1967.

107. Kaffman, M.: "Family Diagnosis and Therapy in Child Emotional Pathology," *Family Process,* 4:241–258, 1965.

108. ————: "Short-Term Family Therapy," *Family Process,* 2:216–234, 1963.

109. Kempler, W.: "Experiential Family Therapy," *International Journal of Group Psychotherapy,* 15:57–71, 1965.

110. ————: "Experiential Psychotherapy with Families," *Family Process,* 7:88–99, 1967.

111. King, C. H.: "Family Therapy with the Deprived Family," *Social Casework,* 48:203–208, 1967.

112. Kohl, R. N.: "Pathologic Reactions of Marital Partners to

Improvement of Patients," *American Journal of Psychiatry,* 118:1036–1041, 1962.

113. Kwiatkowska, H.: "Family Art Therapy," *Family Process,* 6: 37–55, 1967.

114. Laing, R. D., and Esterson, A.: SANITY, MADNESS AND THE FAMILY, Tavistock Publications Ltd., London, 1964.

115. Landes, J., and Winter, W.: "A New Strategy for Treating Disintegrating Families," *Family Process,* 5:1–20, 1966.

116. Laqueur, H. P., and LaBurt, H. A.: "Family Organization on a Modern State Hospital Ward," *Mental Hygiene,* 48:544–551, 1964.

117. Laqueur, H. P.; LaBurt, H. A.; and Morong, E.: "Multiple Family Therapy," in CURRENT PSYCHIATRIC THERAPIES, Vol. 4, J. H. Masserman, ed., Grune & Stratton, Inc., New York, 1964.

118. ———: "Multiple Family Therapy: Further Developments," *International Journal of Social Psychiatry,* Special Edition 2, 70–80, 1964.

119. Lask, E.: "Breaking Down the Walls," *Family Process,* 7:118–125, 1968.

120. Lefer, J.: "Counter-Resistance in Family Therapy," *Journal of Hillside Hospital,* 15:205–210, 1966.

121. Lehrman, N. S.: "The Joint Interview: An Aid to Psychotherapy and Family Stability," *American Journal of Psychotherapy,* 17:83–94, 1963.

122. Liebermann, L. P.: "Joint Interview Technique—An Experiment in Group Psychotherapy," *British Journal of Medical Psychology,* 30:202–207, 1957.

123. Leichter, E., and Shulman, G.: "The Family Interview as an Integrative Device in Group Therapy with Families," *International Journal of Group Psychotherapy,* 13:335–345, 1963.

124. Leveton, A. F.: "Family Therapy as the Treatment of Choice," *Medical Bulletin,* U.S. Army Europe, 21:76–79, 1964.

125. Lidz, T.: THE FAMILY AND HUMAN ADAPTATION, International Universities Press, Inc., New York, 1963.

126. Lidz, T.; Fleck, S.; and Cornelison, A. R.: SCHIZOPHRENIA AND THE FAMILY, International Universities Press, Inc., New York, 1965.

127. Lindberg, D. R., and Wosmek, A. W.: "The Use of Family Sessions in Foster Home Care," *Social Casework,* 44:137–141, 1963.

128. MacGregor, R.: "Multiple Impact Psychotherapy with Families," *Family Process,* 1:15–29, 1962.

129. Markowitz, I.: "Family Therapy in a Child Guidance Clinic," *Psychiatric Quarterly,* 40:308–319, 1966.

130. Martin, F., and Knight, J.: "Joint Interviews as Part of Intake Procedure in a Child Psychiatric Clinic," *Journal of Child Psychology and Psychiatry,* 3:17–26, 1962.

131. Mendell, D., and Fisher, S.: "An Approach to Neurotic Behavior in Terms of a Three-Generation Family Model," *Journal of Nervous and Mental Disease,* 123: 171–180, 1956.

132. Mendell, D.; Cleveland, S. E.; and Fisher, S.: "A Five-Generation Family Theme," *Family Process,* 7:126–132, 1968.

133. Messer, A.: "Family Treatment of a School Phobic Child," *Archives of General Psychiatry,* 11:548–553, 1964.

134. Midelfort, C. F.: THE FAMILY IN PSYCHOTHERAPY, McGraw-Hill Book Co., New York, 1957.

135. ———: "Use of Members of the Family in the Treatment of Schizophrenia," *Family Process,* 1:114–118, 1962.

136. Miller, D., and Westman, J. C.: "Family Teamwork and Psychotherapy," *Family Process,* 5:49–59, 1966.

137. Minuchin, S.: "Family Structure, Family Language, and the Puzzled Therapist," *American Journal of Orthopsychiatry,* 34:347–348, 1964.

138. ———: "Conflict Resolution Family Therapy," *Psychiatry,* 28:278–286, 1965.

139. Minuchin, S.; Auerswald, E.; King, C.; and Rabinowitz, C.: "The Study and Treatment of Families that Produce Multiple Acting-Out Boys," *American Journal of Orthopsychiatry,* 34: 125–134, 1964.

140. Minuchin, S.; Montalvo, B.; Guerney, B. G., Jr.; Rosman, B. L.; and Schurmer, F.: FAMILIES OF THE SLUMS, Basic Books, Inc., New York, 1967.

141. Minuchin, S., and Montalvo, B.: "Techniques for Working with Disorganized, Low Socio-economic Families," *American Journal of Orthopsychiatry,* 37:880–887, 1967.

142. Mitchell, C.: "The Use of Family Sessions in the Diagnosis and Treatment of Disturbances in Children," *Social Casework,* 41: 283–290, 1960.

143. ———: "A Casework Approach to Disturbed Families," in EXPLORING THE BASE FOR FAMILY THERAPY, N. W. Ackerman, F. L. Beatman, and S. N. Sherman, eds., Family Service Association of America, New York, 1961.

144. Mudd, Emily: "Marriage Counseling: A Philosophy and Method," in MAN AND WIVES, A SOURCEBOOK OF FAMILY ATTITUDES, SEXUAL BEHAVIOR AND MARRIAGE COUNSELING, Emily Mudd and A. Kirch, eds. W. W. Norton & Co., Inc., New York, 1957.

145. Osberg, J. W.: "Initial Impressions of the Use of Short-Term Family Group Conferences," *Family Process,* 1:236–244, 1962.

146. Parloff, M. B.: "The Family in Psychotherapy," *Archives of General Psychiatry,* 4:445–451, 1961.

147. Pattison, E. M.: "Treatment of Alcoholic Families with Nurse Home Visits," *Family Process,* 4:75–94, 1965.

148. Patton, J. D.; Bradley, J. D.; and Hornowski, M. J.: "Collaborative Treatment of Marital Partners," *North Carolina Medical Journal,* 19:523–528, 1958.

149. Paul, N. L.: "Effects of Playback on Family Members of Their Own Previously Recorded Conjoint Therapy Material," PSYCHIATRIC RESEARCH REPORT NO. 20, American Psychiatric Association, Washington, D. C., 1966.

150. ———: "The Use of Empathy in the Resolution of Grief," *Perspectives in Biology and Medicine,* 11:153–169, 1967.

151. Paul, N. L., and Grosser, G. H.: "Family Resistance to Change in Schizophrenic Patients," *Family Process,* 3:377–401, 1964.

152. ———: "Operational Mourning and Its Role in Conjoint Family Therapy," *Community Mental Health Journal,* 1:339–345, 1965.

153. Perlmutter, M., et al.: "Family Diagnosis and Therapy Using Videotape Playback," *American Journal of Orthopsychiatry,* 37:900–905, 1967.

154. Pollack, O., and Brieland, D.: "The Midwest Seminar on Family Diagnosis and Treatment," *Social Casework,* 42:319–324, 1961.

155. Rabiner, E. L.: Molinski, H. and Gralnick, A.: "Conjoint Therapy in the Inpatient Setting," *American Journal of Psychotherapy,* 16:618–631, 1962.

156. Ravich, R. A.: "Short-Term Intensive Treatment of Marital Discord," *Voices,* 2:42–48, 1966.

157. Reding, G., and Ennis, B.: "Treatment of the Couple by a Couple," *British Journal of Medical Psychology,* 37:325–330, 1964.

158. Reding, G., and Hoffman, M.: "Treatment of the Couple by a Couple," *British Journal of Medical Psychology,* 40:243–252, 1967.

159. Reidy, J. J.: "An Approach to Family-Centered Treatment in a State Institution," *American Journal of Orthopsychiatry,* 32:133–141, 1962.

160. Ritchie, A.: "Multiple Impact Therapy, an Experiment," *Social Work,* 5:16–21, 1960.

161. Rubinstein, D.: "Family Therapy," in PROGRESS IN NEUROLOGY AND PSYCHIATRY, Vol. 18, E. A. Spiegel, ed., Grune & Stratton, Inc., New York, 1963.

162. Rubinstein, D., and Weiner, O. R.: "Co-Therapy Teamwork Relationships in Family Therapy," in FAMILY THERAPY AND DISTURBED FAMILIES, G. H. Zuk and I. Boszormenyi-Nagy, eds., Science and Behavior Books, Palo Alto, 1967.

163. Sager, C.: "The Development of Marriage Therapy: An Historical Review," *American Journal of Orthopsychiatry,* 36:450–468, 1966.

164. ———: "Transference in Conjoint Treatment of Married Couples," *Archives of General Psychiatry,* 16:185–193, 1967.

165. Satir, V.: "The Quest for Survival: A Training Program for Family Diagnosis and Treatment," *Acta Psychotherapeutica et Psychosomatica,* 11:33–38, 1963.

166. ———: Conjoint Family Therapy, Science and Behavior Books, Palo Alto, 1964.

167. ———: "The Family as a Treatment Unit," *Confinia Psychiatrica Borderland of Psychiatry,* 8:37–42, 1965.

168. Schaffer, L.; Wynne, L. C.; Day, J.; Ryckoff, I. M.; and Halperin, A.: "On the Nature and Sources of the Psychiatrist's Experience with the Family of the Schizophrenic," *Psychiatry,* 25:32–45, 1962.

169. Scheflen, A. E.: Stream and Structure of Communicational Behavior, Eastern Pennsylvania Psychiatric Institute, Behavioral Studies Monograph, No. 1, Philadelphia, 1965.

170. Scherz, F. H.: "Multiple-Client Interviewing: Treatment Implications," *Social Casework,* 43:120–125, 1962.

171. Schuster, F. P.: "Summary Description of Multiple Impact Psychotherapy," *Texas Reports on Biology and Medicine,* 17:426–430, 1959.

172. Searles, H. F.: "Family Treatment and Individual Therapy," in Intensive Family Therapy: Theoretical and Practical Aspects, I. Boszormenyi-Nagy and J. L. Framo, eds., Harper & Row, New York, 1965.

173. Serrano, A. C., and Wilson, N. S.: "Family Therapy in the Treatment of the Brain-Damaged Child," *Diseases of the Nervous System,* 24:732–735, 1963.

173A. Shapiro, R. L.: "The Origin of Adolescent Disturbances in the Family: Some Considerations in Theory and Implications for Therapy," in Family Therapy and Disturbed Families, G. H. Zuk and I. Boszormenyi-Nagy, eds., Science and Behavior Books, Palo Alto, 1967.

174. Shellow, R. S.; Brown, B. S.; and Osberg, J. W.: "Family Group

Therapy in Retrospect: Four Years and Sixty Families," *Family Process,* 2:52–67, 1963.

175. Shereshefsky, P. M.: "Family Unit Treatment in Child Guidance," *Social Casework,* 8:63–70, 1963.

176. Sherman, M. H.; Ackerman, N. W.; Sherman, S. N.; and Mitchell, C.: "Non-Verbal Cues and Re-enactment of Conflict in Family Therapy," *Family Process,* 4:133–162, 1964.

177. Sherman, S. N.: "The Sociopsychological Character of Family-Group Treatment," *Social Casework,* 45:195–201, 1964.

178. Siporin, M.: "Family-Centered Casework in a Psychiatric Setting," *Social Casework,* 37:167–174, 1956.

179. Smith, V. G., and Hepworth, D. H.: "Marriage Counseling with One Marital Partner: Rationale and Clinical Implications," *Social Casework,* 48:352–359, 1967.

180. Sonne, J. C.; Speck, R. V.; and Jungreis, J. E.: "The Absent-Member Maneuver as a Resistance in Family Therapy of Schizophrenia," *Family Process,* 1:44–62, 1962.

181. Sonne, J. C., and Lincoln, G.: "Heterosexual Co-Therapy Team Experience During Family Therapy," *Family Process,* 4:177–197, 1965.

182. Speck, R. V.: "The Home Setting for Family Treatment," *International Journal of Social Psychiatry,* Special Edition 2, 47–53, 1964.

183. ———: "Family Therapy in the Home," *Journal of Marriage and the Family,* 26:72–76, 1964.

184. ———: "Psychotherapy of the Social Network of a Schizophrenic Family," *Family Process,* 6:208–214, 1967.

185. Strean, H. S.: "A Family Therapist Looks at 'Little Hans'," *Family Process,* 6:227–234, 1967.

186. Tharp, R., and Otis, G.: "Toward a Theory for Therapeutic Intervention in Families," *Journal of Consulting Psychology,* 30:426–434, 1966.

187. Tharp, R.: "Marriage Roles, Child Development and Family Treatment," *American Journal of Orthopsychiatry,* 35:531–538, 1965.

188. Thomas, A.: "Simultaneous Psychotherapy with Marital Partners," *American Journal of Psychotherapy,* 10:716–727, 1956.

189. Thormen, G.: FAMILY THERAPY—HELP FOR TROUBLED FAMILIES, Public Affairs Pamphlet No. 356, New York, February, 1964.

190. Treusch, J. V., and Grotjahn, M.: "Psychiatric Family Consultations," *Annals of Internal Medicine,* 66:295–300, 1967.

191. Warkentin, J.: "Psychotherapy with Couples and Families," *Journal of the Medical Association of Georgia,* 49:569–570, 1960.

192. Warkentin, J., and Whitaker, C.: "Serial Impasses in Marriage," PSYCHIATRIC RESEARCH REPORT No. 20, American Psychiatric Association, Washington, D. C., 1966.

193. ————: "The Secret Agenda of the Therapist Doing Couples Therapy," in FAMILY THERAPY AND DISTURBED FAMILIES, G. H. Zuk and I. Boszormenyi-Nagy, eds., Science and Behavior Books, Palo Alto, 1967.

194. Watson, A. S.: "The Conjoint Psychotherapy of Marriage Partners," *American Journal of Orthopsychiatry,* 33:912–923, 1963.

195. Whitaker, C.: "Psychotherapy with Couples," *American Journal of Psychotherapy,* 12:18–23, 1958.

196. Whitaker, C.; Felder, R. E.; and Warkentin, J.: "Countertransference in the Family Treatment of Schizophrenia," in INTENSIVE FAMILY THERAPY: THEORETICAL AND PRACTICAL ASPECTS, I. Boszormenyi-Nagy and J. L. Framo, eds., Harper & Row, New York, 1965.

197. Wilkinson, C., and Reed, C.: "An Approach to the Family Therapy Process," *Diseases of the Nervous System,* 26:705–714, 1965.

198. Williams, F.: "Family Therapy: A Critical Assessment," *American Journal of Orthopsychiatry,* 37:912–919, 1967.

199. Wyatt, G. L., and Herzan, H. M.: "Therapy with Stuttering Children and Their Mothers," *American Journal of Orthopsychiatry,* 32:645–659, 1962.

200. Wynne, L. C.: "Some Indications and Contraindications for Ex-

ploratory Family Therapy," in INTENSIVE FAMILY THERAPY: THEORETICAL AND PRACTICAL ASPECTS, I. Boszormenyi-Nagy and J. L. Framo, eds., Harper & Row, New York, 1965.

201. ————: "The Study of Intrafamilial Alignments and Splits in Exploratory Family Therapy," in EXPLORING THE BASE FOR FAMILY THERAPY, N. W. Ackerman, F. L. Beatman, and S. N. Sherman, eds., Family Service Association of America, New York, 1961.

202. Zierer, E.; Sternberg, D.; Finn, R.; and Farmer, N.: "Family Creative Analysis: Its Role in Treatment," *Bulletin of Art Therapy,* 5:87–104, 1906.

203. Zuk, G. H.: "Preliminary Study of the Go-Between Process in Family Therapy," in PROCEEDINGS OF THE 73RD ANNUAL CONVENTION, American Psychological Association, Chicago, 1965.

204. ————: "Family Therapy," *Archives of General Psychiatry,* 16:71–79, 1967.

205. Zuk, G. H., and Boszormenyi-Nagy, I., eds.: FAMILY THERAPY AND DISTURBED FAMILIES, Science and Behavior Books, Palo Alto, 1966.

206. Zuk, G. H., and Rubinstein, D.: "A Review of Concepts in the Study and Treatment of Families of Schizophrenics," in INTENSIVE FAMILY THERAPY: THEORETICAL AND PRACTICAL ASPECTS, I. Boszormenyi-Nagy and J. L. Framo, eds., Harper & Row, New York, 1965.

207. Zwerling, I., and Mendelsohn, M.: "Initial Family Reactions to Day Hospitalization," *Family Process,* 4:50–63, 1965.

Appendix 2

FAMILY THERAPY QUESTIONNAIRE

Prepared by

<small>THE COMMITTEE ON THE FAMILY</small>
GROUP FOR THE ADVANCEMENT OF PSYCHIATRY

Members:

Murray Bowen, M.D.
David Mendell, M.D.
Ivan Boszormenyi-Nagy, M.D.
Norman L. Paul, M.D.
Joseph Satten, M.D.

Kurt O. Schlesinger, M.D.
John P. Spiegel, M.D.
Lyman C. Wynne, M.D., Ph.D.
Israel Zwerling, M.D., Ph.D.,
                                    Chairman

Consultants:

Alice R. Cornelison, M.S.W.
Jay Haley, M.A.

Florence Kluckhohn, Ph.D.
Celia Mitchell, A.C.S.W.

IDENTIFYING DATA

Name_____ Address_____

                                                    Religious
Profession_____ Age____ Sex____ Affiliation_____

Professional Organizations to which you belong:

_____

_____

SECTION I: *Factors Related to Therapist's Route to Family Therapy*

I:1   Which of the following circumstances were associated with your
interest in doing family therapy? Check as many items as are
applicable.

Entirely independent decision (e.g., via having worked
with several individuals of one family)............... _____

Training program offered during graduate or post graduate work... _____

Invitation from colleagues to join in exploring family
therapy... _____

Lecture or paper on family therapy................... _____

Watching a family therapist work.................... _____

Other (specify)_____

If your starting point was a training program, please identify and
describe it briefly:_____

625

If your starting point was a group of colleagues, please describe the setting briefly:_____

_____

I:2   Please *rank* each of the following factors in the order of their impor-
        tance in influencing you to do family therapy: use "0" for all factors
        which have played essentially no role, and then use "1" for the factor
        which most influenced you, "2" for the factor which influenced you
        next most, etc.

        Previous work with group therapy   _____
        Previous work with children and parents   _____
        Previous work with schizophrenic patients   _____
        Dissatisfaction with results of individual therapy   _____
        Desire to treat people more efficiently   _____
        Pre-existing interest in marriage and family   _____
        General experimental curiosity   _____
        Other (specify)_____

        _____

I:3   List in order of importance the individuals who have offered theories
        about families which most influenced your work.
        1. _____   3. _____
        2. _____   4. _____

I:4   Where did you first hear or read about family therapy in a way that
        made a deep impression on you?_____

        _____

I:5   Do you think that you will continue doing family therapy or do you
        regard this work as a temporary phase in your career?
        Temporary_____   Continue_____
        Please say why:_____

SECTION II: *Factors Related to Routes of Families into Family Therapy*

II:1 A. How many of the following units are currently in therapy or counseling with you at least one hour weekly?

	Families	Couples*	Individ-uals**	Unrelated Person Therapy Groups
In Private Practice	_____	_____	_____	_____
In a Research Project	_____	_____	_____	_____
Training Project	_____	_____	_____	_____
School Setting	_____	_____	_____	_____
Pastoral Setting	_____	_____	_____	_____
Mental Health Facility	_____	_____	_____	_____
Other (specify)_____				

B. How many did you see for diagnostic evaluation in the past 12 months?

II:2 If you work at least part time in a mental health facility, please check what kind it is in the list below and state your position and the number of hours per week you work there (multiple items may be checked as they apply):

A. *Setting*	*Position*	*Hours per week*
State Mental Hospital	_____	_____
Municipal Mental Hospital	_____	_____
Private Mental Hospital	_____	_____
Veterans Administration Hosp.	_____	_____
Armed Forces Hospital	_____	_____
Community Mental Health Cent.	_____	_____
College Psychiatric Service	_____	_____
Court Clinic	_____	_____
Industrial Psychiatric Service	_____	_____
Child Guidance Clinic	_____	_____
Family Service Agency	_____	_____
Other Hospital (please specify):	_____	_____

---

* "Couples" refers to parents seen together, but without their children. Childless couples are to be counted as "Families."

** "Individuals" refers to persons seen alone in individual therapy, and not to individuals seen as part of a program of family therapy.

			Hours per week
II:2	B. *Type of Service*	*Position*	
	Inpatient Service	_____	_____
	Outpatient Service	_____	_____
	Day Hospital	_____	_____
	Evening Hospital	_____	_____
	Day Care Unit	_____	_____
	Emergency or Walk-In Service	_____	_____
	Home Care Unit or Service	_____	_____
	Halfway House or Service	_____	_____
	Other (please specify):_____		

II:3   Of the families and couples in family treatment with you at this time, what were the referral sources? Please check the approximate percentage from the sources listed:

Medical Sources	*More than 50%*	*25 to 50%*	*Less than 25%*
Psychoanalyst	_____	_____	_____
Psychiatrist	_____	_____	_____
General Practitioner	_____	_____	_____
Pediatrician	_____	_____	_____
Internist	_____	_____	_____
Hospital Personnel	_____	_____	_____
Other (please specify)	_____		

Community Sources			
Social Work Agency			
Family Agency	_____	_____	_____
Children's Agency	_____	_____	_____
Residential Center	_____	_____	_____
School	_____	_____	_____
Church	_____	_____	_____
Community Center	_____	_____	_____
Individual Social Worker	_____	_____	_____
Individual Psychologist	_____	_____	_____
Police or Court	_____	_____	_____
Clinic	_____	_____	_____
Other (please specify)	_____		

II:3 If you have noticed an out-of-the-ordinary increase or decrease in frequency of referral from any of these sources in the past year, would you please describe?

_____

_____

II:4 Of the families in treatment with you in the last year, in what percentage was *family* therapy decided upon?:

% of Families

A. Because of your evaluation of the presenting problem? _____

B. Because individual treatment developed into family therapy? _____

C. Because treatment of marital pair developed into family therapy? _____

D. Because families requested treatment of the family as a group? _____

E. If any families requested treatment as a family, where did they learn about this form of treatment? Please check as many as apply:

Newspaper or journals............... _____

Radio or TV....................... _____

Other families in treatment.......... _____

Other (please specify):_____

II:5 We are interested in the prior treatment experience of families currently in treatment. Please estimate what percent of families in family treatment with you this last year had prior treatment in the following categories; and indicate for those who had any form of treatment how successful it was reported to have been:

	More than 50%	25% to 50%	Less than 25%	Helped substantially	Helped moderately	Treatment failure
A. No prior treatment for any member	____	____	____	____	____	____
B. Prior treatment:						
i. For one family member	____	____	____	____	____	____
ii. Individual treatment for more than one member	____	____	____	____	____	____
iii. Conjoint marital treatment	____	____	____	____	____	____
iv. Family therapy	____	____	____	____	____	____
v. Group therapy	____	____	____	____	____	____

SECTION III: *Family Therapy Training*

III:1   Has your interest in family work dictated a
         change in jobs for you during the past 4 years?   Yes_____ No___
             If yes, was antagonism to family work on the
             previous job a factor in the change of job?   Yes_____ No_____
             If yes, would you describe briefly:_____
         _____

III:2   A. Does any organization or institute with which you are
            affiliated offer formal training in the practice of family
            therapy?   Yes_____
                                                                        No_____
                If yes, please name the organization:_____
            _____

         B. Are there informal training exercises? Please check any of the
            items below which apply:
                i. Family research projects are in progress......... _____
               ii. Family therapy cases are presented at some clinical
                   case conferences............................. _____
               iii. Therapists doing family therapy meet to discuss
                   their cases................................. _____
               iv. Other educational or training activities.......... _____
                   Specify _____
                   _____

                None of the above........................ _____
III:3   Are you currently in training in family therapy?:   Yes_____
                                                                     No_____
             If yes, are you in:
             Formal training   _____
             Informal training _____
             If you are in training, do you have supervision in your work with
             families or couples?
             A great deal   _____
             A small amount   _____
             None   _____
III:4   Do you teach family therapy?   Yes _____
                                                                    No _____

         If you teach family therapy, do you teach by the following methods
         (multiple items may be checked):
             Lectures   _____
             Case seminars   _____
             Supervision   _____
             Demonstration   _____
             Audio-Visual materials _____
             Other (please specify) _____
         _____

III:5   Since we would like to pick up trends in attitudes about family
        therapy, would you give your impression about the attitudes of the
        colleagues in your locale toward work with couples or families. *In
        the last year*, has the attitude among your colleagues toward the
        practice of family therapy been:
        One of increasing acceptance   _____
        One of increasing antagonism   _____
        No particular change   _____
        Comments: _____

SECTION IV: *Some Demographic Characteristics of Families in Family Therapy*

IV:1   Please rank in order the socio-economic levels in which your popula-
        tion of patients mainly fall. Place a (0) next to any which do not apply
        to any of your patients, a (1) by the most frequent, a (2) by the next
        most frequent and so on.
        Executive and major professional................... _____
        Junior executive, minor professional, and small business
            ownership..................................... _____
        Clerical and sales............................... _____
        Skilled labor.................................... _____
        Unskilled labor.................................. _____
        Don't know...................................... _____

IV:2   Please indicate the approximate percentages of your patients with
        regard to racial, ethnic or national grouping:
        A. Negro   _____   White   _____   Oriental   _____
        B. Anglo-Saxon _____   Mexican   _____   Other (specify)_____
           Irish   _____   Italian   _____   _____
                                  Central
           Puerto Rican _____   European _____

IV:3   Please list the proportions of your population of families which fall
        into the major religious backgrounds.
        Protestant _____   Jewish   _____
        Catholic   _____   Other   _____
                                Don't know _____

IV:4   Are the following religious elements of importance in your work with
        families?
        Religious values   Yes   _____
                            No   _____
                            Don't know _____
        Religious conflicts Yes   _____
                            No   _____
                            Don't know _____

IV:5   Of the population of labelled patients (or problem family members) in your care during the calendar year, please indicate roughly what proportion are:
Children _____   Middle aged _____
Adolescents _____   Elderly _____
Young Adolescents _____

IV:6   Of the families in treatment with you in the last year, please rank the following diagnoses in terms of frequency. Place a (1) if the diagnosis is most frequent, a (2) for the diagnosis next most frequent, and so on.
Depression _____   Psychotic symptoms _____
Neurotic symptoms _____   Mental retardation _____
Character disorders _____

SECTION V: *Techniques and Practices*

V:1   A. Where do you see the families you treat? Please check as many lines as are applicable:

Place	Always	Usually	Some-times	Never
In your office				
In the family home				
Other (specify)				

B. If you see the family in the office, have you made one or more home visits in the last year? Yes _____ No _____

V:2   A. How many therapists are in the room with the family?

	Always	Usually	Some-times	Never
You alone				
Two therapists				
More than two				
Other (e.g., an observer)				
i. If there are two therapists are they				
both male				
both female				
male and female				
ii. If there are two therapists the function of the 2nd is considered				
co-therapist				
recorder				

		Always	Usually	Some-times	Never
V:2	supervisor	___	___	___	___
	trainee	___	___	___	___
	observer	___	___	___	___

iii. If two therapists are in the room, the two professional disciplines are _____ and _____

iv. If two therapists are in the room, which one of the two statements applies?

☐ 1. One of the therapists is considered in charge.

☐ 2. Both are considered of equal rank.

	Always	Usually	Some-times	Never
If two therapists are in the room and disagree, do you				
1. Acknowledge the disagreement in the presence of the family?	___	___	___	___
2. Work out the differences outside the treatment session?	___	___	___	___
3. Argue out the disagreement in the session?	___	___	___	___

4. Please describe any special aspect of your approach to handling disagreements between therapists: _____

_____

_____

V:2	B. If two therapists are used at any time, do you	Always	Usually	Some-times	Never
	1. Continue with the same two therapists?	___	___	___	___
	2. Change one of the two therapists?	___	___	___	___
	3. Change to one therapists?	___	___	___	___

V:3	A. In your program of family therapy do you	Always	Usually	Some-times	Never
	1. Have no scheduled sessions with any individual family member?	___	___	___	___
	2. See the family and also schedule sessions with an individual member of the family alone?	___	___	___	___
	3. Have another therapist see individual members of a family you are treating?	___	___	___	___

			Some-times	Never

V:4   A. Is it your policy to see all family
      members in every session?

	Always	Usually	Some-times	Never
A. Is it your policy to see all family members in every session?	___	___	___	___
i. If your answer is always, do you ever relax this policy on clinical grounds?	___	___	___	___
ii. Do you hold sessions if some family members are absent?	___	___	___	___

B. When you treat the family do you include:

	Always	Usually	Some-times	Never
i. Only the parents?	___	___	___	___
ii. Only the nuclear family of parents and children?	___	___	___	___
iii. Nuclear family plus other persons living in the household?	___	___	___	___
iv. Extended significant kin living outside the household?	___	___	___	___
v. Significant non-family members?	___	___	___	___

V:5   A. How frequently does each description apply to your family treatment procedure?

	Always	Usually	Some-times	Never
i. See all family members together throughout treatment?	___	___	___	___
ii. See all family members for 1 or more initial evaluative sessions and then shift to only a segment of the family?	___	___	___	___
iii. See all family members for 1 or more initial evaluative sessions and shift to a single individual?	___	___	___	___
iv. See all family members and shift to the marital pair?	___	___	___	___
v. See individual members initially and then shift to the whole family?	___	___	___	___
vi. See individual members initially and shift to the marital pair?	___	___	___	___
vii. Other (please specify)	___	___	___	___

V:6	With reference to frequency do you schedule family sessions:	Always	Usually	Some-times	Never
	1. Less than once a week	____	____	____	____
	2. Once a week	____	____	____	____
	3. Twice a week	____	____	____	____
	4. More than twice a week	____	____	____	____

V:7	The duration of family sessions is:	Always	Usually	Some-times	Never
	A. Less than 50 minutes	____	____	____	____
	B. 50–60 minutes	____	____	____	____
	C. More than 1 hour but less than 2 hours	____	____	____	____
	D. 2 hours or more	____	____	____	____

V:8	Which of the following most typically describes the way you prefer to work during the course of treatment?:	Always	Usually	Some-times	Never
	A. i. Attempt long-term treatment with families	____	____	____	____
	ii. Attempt brief treatment with families	____	____	____	____
	B. i. See a family for a short time and then recess them and see them again for a short time	____	____	____	____
	ii. See the family regularly until the problems are resolved	____	____	____	____

V:9	Do you see families in private practice unobserved?	Always	Usually	Some-times	Never
		____	____	____	____
	Do you observe the family treatment of other therapists?	____	____	____	____

Is your family therapy usually observed by others?   Yes_____   No_____

If yes, is it for:
Supervision _____
Training   _____
Research   _____
Other (specify)_____

_____

_____
_____
_____

	Always	Usually	Some-times	Never

V:10   Do you record your family session
        on tape or film?

        If you record, are the recordings used
        In your own supervision
        In your supervision of others
        For group discussion among your
            peers
        For confrontation of the family
            unit
        Other_____

        Have you been filmed or videotaped with a
        family?   Yes____   No____
        If you have been filmed or videotaped with a
        family was it at:
        Diagnostic session   _____
        Ongoing treatment session _____
        Do you usually play tape recordings of films
        back to a family during their treatment ses-
        sion?   Yes____   No____
        Do you ever have family members take tape
        recordings home to listen to?   Yes____   No____

V:11   If you do family therapy in private practice, do you charge
        for family treatment:
            The same rate per unit of time as individual treatment _____
            A higher rate than individual treatment............. _____
            Other_____
            _____
            _____

V:12   In the last year, have you treated a family in
        which a member was hospitalized?   Yes____   No____
            If yes, about how many families? _____
        If you have treated families in which one
        member was hospitalized, would you say the
        hospital staff has been:
            Cooperative with you   _____
            A problem for your treatment _____
            Other_____
            _____
            _____

V:13   A. Do you use drugs as part of your family treatment:
          ☐ Always ☐ Usually ☐ Sometimes ☐ Never

      B. If you do use drugs
          i. Do you prescribe them yourself?   ☐ Yes ☐ No
         ii. Do you delegate prescription to someone
            else?   ☐ Yes ☐ No
        iii. Do you most frequently use drugs on your own initiative ☐,
            or at the insistence of the family ☐ ?
        iv. Do you use drugs only for the identified patient ☐, or for
            other family members as well ☐ ?
         v. In your experience, do drugs facilitate family therapy ☐,
            impede family therapy ☐, or have no consistent impact on
            family therapy ☐ ?
        vi. Please comment briefly on special problems created by the
            use of drugs in family therapy:_____
            _____
            _____

V:14   When you are dealing with a family in which
      one member is identified as "the patient" do
      you:
      1. Require that other family members con-
         cede they are patients too at the start of
         treatment?   Yes____   No____
      2. Let the process of treatment work out the
         labelling of other family members as pa-
         tients?   Yes____   No____
      3. Ignore the labelling process?   Yes____   No____
      4. Other_____

V:15   Do you see more than one family together in
      a group?   Yes____   No____
        If yes, how many families do you usually
          see in a group?   _____
        If yes, do you also have regular treatment
          sessions with single families?   Yes____   No____

V:16   A. How would you best describe   *Some-*
        the way you work with a family? *Always Usually times Never*
         i. Indicate to family members
           how to respond in the room,
           such as expressing their ideas
           and feelings, but not give
           them instructions how to be-
           have outside the room   ____   ____   ____   ____

		Always	Usually	Some-times	Never

V:16   A. ii. Indicate to families how to behave in the room and also give them instructions to follow outside the room

Always	Usually	Some-times	Never
____	____	____	____

iii. If you give instructions about behavior outside the room is it typically direct advice on how to behave more sensibly

____	____	____	____

iv. Indirect suggestions designed to induce a change

____	____	____ `	____

v. Other (specify)_____

B. Do you set limits on how family members are to behave in the room, such as controlling children or forbidding certain topics?

Always	Usually	Some-times	Never
____	____	____	____

When in a room with family members, do you:

i. Consistently encourage them to talk to each other rather than to you?

____	____	____	____

ii. Consistently encourage the members to take turns talking to you?

____	____	____	____

iii. Allow family members to talk to each other and you?

____	____	____	____

C. Please check each item with regard to the frequency with which it applies to your treatment of families:

Always	Usually	Some-times	Never

i. You give advice

____	____	____	____

ii. You discuss transference explicitly

____	____	____	____

iii. You remain neutral in relation to family factions

____	____	____	____

iv. You take sides in family factions

____	____	____	____

v. You discuss your own feelings aroused in family sessions

____	____	____	____

vi. You attempt to relate the past of family members to the present

____	____	____	____

V:17   A. Which statement below best describes the way you typically deal with sexual matters in treatment sessions:

Never discuss sex at all........................ _____

Discuss any aspect of sex with children present.... _____

Exclude the children when sex comes up as a topic _____

Exclude the children when the parents' personal sex life is the topic, but not when sex in general is discussed.................................... _____

Other_____

    B. Do you take a position on extra-marital relationships of either or both partners while they are in treatment?   ☐ Yes   ☐ No

If yes, please describe briefly_____

_____

V:18   When introducing family therapy to families, which of the following is the usual way you label the process to them:

Therapy   _____

Treatment   _____

Counseling   _____

Education   _____

No label   _____

Other (please name) _____

V:19   Do you ever see families who are "ordered" into treatment, as when a judge requires it of them?   Yes_____   No_____

If yes, under what circumstances?_____

V:20   Would you accept a family in treatment if one of the family members was concurrently in individual treatment with someone else?   Yes_____   No_____

If yes, would you accept a family in treatment if one of the family members was concurrently in treatment with someone else and that therapist opposed his patient entering family therapy?   Yes_____   No_____

V:21   Do you consider family therapy an alternative to hospitalization in cases of:

Suicidal threat   Yes_____   No_____

Acting out   Yes_____   No_____

Threats of violence   Yes_____   No_____

V:22   Which of the following statements seem to apply to your attitude about family therapy: Please check only *one*.

Family therapy is the method of choice over other methods of psychotherapy. . . . . _____

Family therapy is the method of choice but only in combination with individual therapy. . . . . _____

Family therapy alone is a useful method. . . . . _____

Family therapy is a useful method if combined with other methods of therapy. . . . . _____

SECTION VI: *Indications and Evaluations*

VI:1   Many variables play a role in determining goals of family therapy including the starting position of the family, the availability of time both with regard to frequency and duration of therapy, etc. Please check the *one or two boxes* for each goal listed which best apply to what you are *actually doing now, or have actually done recently with families in treatment.*

Kind of change	PRIMARY GOALS		SECONDARY GOALS		
	With all families	*With certain families*	*With all families*	*With certain families*	*Rarely or never a goal with any family*
I More flexible assumption of leadership by any family member as circumstances require					
II Improved clarity of communication within the family					
III Improved autonomy and individuation of family members					
IV Symptomatic improvement in one or more family members					

V Improved empathy between family members					
VI Improved task performance by one or more members (e.g., school performance of a child, work performance of a parent)					
VII Improved agreement about roles taken by family members					
VIII Reduction of quarreling and conflict within the family.					

VI:2   For each of the issues or questions related to the decision to use family treatment indicated below, please check the boxes which apply:

		I do take this issue or question into consideration and my reason for deciding upon family treatment is based upon:		
Question or issue	*I do not consider this issue or question*	*Impressions from clinical experience*	*Regular discussions with colleagues*	*Research interests*
I Indications and contraindications for family treatment				
II Type of difficulties in family relationships which are appropriately treated with a family approach				
III Type of symptomatic problems or "diagnosis" which are suitable for treatment with a family approach				

IV Relevance of kind of social class, cultural or religious background of family regarding suitability for a family approach				
V Comparing outcome of individual and family approaches for treatment of similar problems				
VI Comparing outcome of conventional group therapy and family therapy for treatment of similar problems				
VII Change taking place after family treatment ended (follow-up assessment)				
VIII How symptoms or problems shift from one family member to another during course of therapy				
IX How different kinds of intervention affect processes of therapy				
X How using one therapist versus two or more affects outcome				
XI How frequency of sessions affects outcome				
XII How combining individual therapy with family therapy affects outcome				

SECTION VII: *Conceptual Framework*

VII:1   If you use the health-illness framework, how do you conceptualize health and illness when working with the family? Do you consider: *Always Usually Some-times Never*

A. One or several members sick, and the others needed in therapy to help the sick one?   _____ _____ _____ _____

B. Both patient and family "sick"?   _____ _____ _____ _____

C. The family as a system is the significant factor in the illness shown in individuals?   _____ _____ _____ _____

VII:2   What other model do you use instead of or in addition to the health-sickness framework? (e.g., religious, social competence, role theory, etc.)_____

VII:3   What theoretical position or concept do you find of use in family
          therapy?

	Name of Principal Theorist(s) used	Always	Usually	Some-times	Never
A. Psychodynamic	————	———	———	———	———
B. Behavior	————	———	———	———	———
C. Learning	————	———	———	———	———
D. Theory of Small Groups	————	———	———	———	———
E. Family Theory	————	———	———	———	———
F. Existential	————	———	———	———	———
G. Other (specify)	————	———	———	———	———
	————	———	———	———	———
	————	———	———	———	———

SECTION VIII: *Ethical Issues*

VIII:1   Have you ever encountered value
          conflicts in your family work?   *Always Usually* Some-times *Never*

A. Between family members
B. Between therapist and one family member
C. Between therapist and all but one family member
D. Between therapist and entire family
E. Other_____

VIII:2   Please specify the most frequent value conflicts you have found in
          treating families._____
          _____
          _____

VIII:3   How do you deal with secrets and
          confidentiality in family work?   *Always Usually* Some-times *Never*

A. Maintain confidences?
B. Share them with other family members?
C. Refuse to hear individual communications?

VIII:4   Please describe briefly how you tried to resolve problems arising
          from secrets._____
          _____
          _____
          _____

VIII:5   Do you see any differences in these issues as they arise in family
         therapy as contrasted with individual therapy? Please describe.

         _____

         Please list your publications on family (1) therapy, (2) research,
         (3) theory, and (4) assessment.

         Any comments you can make about the experience of filling out this
         questionnaire will be appreciated.

Acknowledgments

The program of the Group for the Advancement of Psychiatry, a non-profit, tax-exempt organization, is made possible largely through the voluntary contributions and efforts of its members. For their financial assistance during the past fiscal year, in helping it to fulfill its aims, GAP is grateful to the following foundations and organizations:

Sponsors

THE COMMONWEALTH FUND
THE DIVISION FUND
MAURICE FALK MEDICAL FUND
THE GRANT FOUNDATION
THE GROVE FOUNDATION
THE HOLZHEIMER FUND
ITTLESON FAMILY FOUNDATION
THE OLIN FOUNDATION
OPPENHEIMER & CO. FOUNDATION, INC.
A. H. ROBINS COMPANY
ROCHE LABORATORIES
SANDOZ PHARMACEUTICALS
THE MURRAY L. SILBERSTEIN FUND
SQUIBB INSTITUTE FOR MEDICAL RESEARCH
SMITH KLINE & FRENCH FOUNDATION
THE UPJOHN COMPANY
WALLACE PHARMACEUTICALS
WYETH LABORATORIES

Donors

VIRGINIA & NATHAN BEDERMAN FOUNDATION
THE GRALNICK FOUNDATION
THE FOREST HOSPITAL FOUNDATION

Publications of the
Group for the Advancement of Psychiatry

Because readers of this publication may not be aware of previously published GAP titles, a selected listing is given below:

Number	Title	Price
27A	INTEGRATION AND CONFLICT IN FAMILY BEHAVIOR —Aug. 1954; reissued June 1968	$1.50
45	CONFIDENTIALITY AND PRIVILEGED COMMUNICATION IN THE PRACTICE OF PSYCHIATRY—June 1960	.75
49	REPORTS IN PSYCHOTHERAPY: INITIAL INTERVIEWS —June 1961	.75
58	MEDICAL PRACTICE AND PSYCHIATRY: THE IMPACT OF CHANGING DEMANDS—Oct. 1964	.75
63	PSYCHIATRIC RESEARCH AND THE ASSESSMENT OF CHANGE—Nov. 1966	2.50
68	THE PSYCHIC FUNCTION OF RELIGION IN MENTAL ILLNESS AND HEALTH—Jan. 1968	1.50
71	ON PSYCHOTHERAPY AND CASEWORK (A POSITION STATEMENT)—Oct. 1968	1.00
73	PSYCHOTHERAPY AND THE DUAL RESEARCH TRADITION —October 1969	1.50
76	THE CASE HISTORY METHOD IN THE STUDY OF FAMILY PROCESS—March 1970	4.00

Orders amounting to less than $3.00 must be accompanied by remittance. All prices are subject to change without notice.

GAP publications may be ordered on a subscription basis. The current subscription cycle comprising the Volume 7 Series covers the period from July 1, 1968 to June 30, 1971. The subscription fee is $12.00 U.S.A. and $13.00 Canadian and other foreign, payable in U.S. currency.

Bound volumes of GAP publications issued since 1947 are also available. They include GAP titles no longer in print that are unavailable in any other form.

Please send your order and remittance to: Publications Office, Group for the Advancement of Psychiatry, 419 Park Avenue South, New York, New York 10016.

This publication was produced for the Group for the Advancement of Psychiatry by the Mental Health Materials Center, Inc., New York.